JUVENILE JUSTICE
AND
CHILDREN'S LAW

2nd Edition

by
Margaret C. Jasper

Oceana's Legal Almanac Series
Law for the Layperson

2001
Oceana Publications, Inc.
Dobbs Ferry, New York

Information contained in this work has been obtained by Oceana Publications from sources believed to be reliable. However, neither the Publisher nor its authors guarantee the accuracy or completeness of any information published herein, and neither Oceana nor its authors shall be responsible for any errors, omissions or damages arising from the use of this information. This work is published with the understanding that Oceana and its authors are supplying information, but are not attempting to render legal or other professional services. If such services are required, the assistance of an appropriate professional should be sought.

Library of Congress Control Number: 2001132451

ISBN 0-379-11356-2

Oceana's Legal Almanac Series: Law for the Layperson
ISSN 1075-7376

©2001 by Oceana Publications, Inc.

Manufactured in the United States of America on acid-free paper.

To My Husband Chris

**Your love and support
are my motivation and inspiration**

-and-

In memory of my son, Jimmy

Table of Contents

CHAPTER 6:
EMANCIPATION

CHAPTER 7:
TEENAGE PREGNANCY

CHAPTER 8:
ADDITIONAL AGE-RELATED ISSUES AND RESTRICTIONS

APPENDICES

ABOUT THE AUTHOR

MARGARET C. JASPER is an attorney engaged in the general practice of law in South Salem, New York, concentrating in the areas of personal injury and entertainment law. Ms. Jasper holds a Juris Doctor degree from Pace University School of Law, White Plains, New York, is a member of the New York and Connecticut bars, and is certified to practice before the United States District Courts for the Southern and Eastern Districts of New York, and the United States Supreme Court.

Ms. Jasper has been appointed to the panel of arbitrators of the American Arbitration Association and the law guardian panel for the Family Court of the State of New York, is a member of the Association of Trial Lawyers of America, and is a New York State licensed real estate broker and member of the Westchester County Board of Realtors, operating as Jasper Real Estate, in South Salem, New York.

Ms. Jasper is the author and general editor of the following legal almanacs: Juvenile Justice and Children's Law; Marriage and Divorce; Estate Planning; The Law of Contracts; The Law of Dispute Resolution; Law for the Small Business Owner; The Law of Personal Injury; Real Estate Law for the Homeowner and Broker; Everyday Legal Forms; Dictionary of Selected Legal Terms; The Law of Medical Malpractice; The Law of Product Liability; The Law of No-Fault Insurance; The Law of Immigration; The Law of Libel and Slander; The Law of Buying and Selling; Elder Law; The Right to Die; AIDS Law; The Law of Obscenity and Pornography; The Law of Child Custody; The Law of Debt Collection; Consumer Rights Law; Bankruptcy Law for the Individual Debtor; Victim's Rights Law; Animal Rights Law; Workers' Compensation Law; Employee Rights in the Workplace; Probate Law; Environmental Law; Labor Law; The Americans with Disabilities Act; The Law of Capital Punishment; Education Law; The Law of Violence Against Women; Landlord-Tenant Law; Insurance Law; Religion and the Law; Commercial Law; Motor Vehicle Law; Social Security Law; The Law of Drunk Driving; The Law of Speech and the First Amendment;

Employment Discrimination Under Title VII; Hospital Liability Law; Home Mortgage Law Primer; Copyright Law; Patent Law; Trademark Law; Special Education Law; The Law of Attachment and Garnishment; Banks and their Customers; and Credit Cards and the Law.

INTRODUCTION

The future of our society is in our children. This places a tremendous responsibility on adults to make sure that the children in our society receive the proper care, treatment and protection they need in order to carry this torch. The duties to nurture and instill positive values in children primarily fall upon the shoulders of their parents and families.

Unfortunately, not all children have the advantage of being brought up in a positive and loving environment, in which case society must intervene and attempt to rescue those children. Most often, when the family fails, responsibility is shifted to the educational system, social services programs, the police department and the juvenile court system to respond to the needs of the children who have "fallen through the cracks."

The problems and concerns involved in caring for and disciplining children are certainly not new. As long as there have been children on this earth, there have been adults wondering how best to care for them. How do we protect children from irresponsible parents? At what point must society intervene as a surrogate caretaker? How do we discipline children when they do something wrong? At what age should children be held responsible for their actions? At what age are children mature enough to handle their own affairs? The questions are endless as well as timeless.

This legal almanac explores the various methods society has devised to protect, educate and discipline its children, both historically and currently. It defines and discusses the role of the juvenile justice system in guiding and disciplining wayward youth, and protecting abused and neglected children, and the safeguards which have been devised to ensure that the children who enter the system are afforded their constitutional rights.

Finally, this almanac discusses areas of great concern affecting youth today, including teenage violence, illegal drug and alcohol abuse, suicide, underage drinking and driving, and the various state statutes relating to age and the ability of children to handle their own affairs and make their own decisions.

The Appendix provides tables identifying relevant statutes, and other pertinent information and data. The Glossary contains definitions of many of the basic legal terms used throughout the almanac.

CHAPTER 1:
THE JUVENILE JUSTICE SYSTEM

HISTORICAL OVERVIEW

Juvenile Justice and English Common Law

It is important to understand the history of juvenile justice under the English common law because it is at the heart of our own juvenile justice system.

By the eighteenth century, a set of rules concerning the liability of a child to commit a crime was established, and juveniles enjoyed certain protections from criminal prosecution, depending on their age. For example, children under 7 were absolutely immune from criminal prosecution. Children under 14 were presumed to lack criminal intent, and thus a child could not be found guilty of a crime without incontrovertible evidence that the child clearly understood the consequences of his or her act.

The infancy presumption was not applicable to the older child—aged 14 to 21—and they were held accountable for their crimes as adults. Nevertheless, the available criminal penalties under English common law were often inapplicable to those children. For example, forfeiture of property was a common penalty assessed against a convicted person. Because English law prohibited a person under the age of 21 from owning property, however, this form of punishment was unavailable.

Although capital punishment existed as a penalty for felony convictions, juveniles were rarely sentenced to execution, their age being a mitigating factor. One form of punishment which was used for juveniles was transportation—banishment from the country.

Evolution of American Juvenile Justice

In early colonial America, the discipline of children was carried out by the family, community and church. Discipline was strict, and punishment was severe and physically administered. Parents were required by law to control and discipline their children, and they did so by whatever means necessary. Whippings were customary. Nevertheless, if the parents failed to control the child, he or she was placed with another family who was deemed better able to handle this responsibility, and for whom the child was required to work.

Corporal punishment—also known as "beating the devil" out of the wrongdoer—was utilized until the early 1800's, when it became unpopular and even banned in some states. Juries became reluctant to convict juvenile offenders, who were often sentenced to adult prisons, because of the lack of appropriate punishments and available facilities. In addition, there was no distinction between children who had actually committed a crime and children who were either dependent or neglected, such as orphans, runaways and abused or neglected children.

Prior to urbanization, mass immigration and the industrial revolution, there was very little crime in America. With such rapid changes came an increase in poverty, the advent of slums, and the exploitation of children for cheap labor. Prior to industrialization, primarily due to a lack of transportable goods, there was very little "property crime"—crime involving the theft of property, such as burglary and robbery.

After industrialization, people began to accumulate property that was moveable and, therefore, "stealable," and property crimes became a big problem in nineteenth century America, as they are to this day. This greatly contributed to the rising number of juvenile lawbreakers because, statistically, juvenile offenders have always been found to commit a disproportionate number of property crimes.

In the 1820's, in response to this new wave of juvenile crime, an attempt to reform the way troubled children were treated began, and institutions to house juvenile delinquents separate from adults were founded. Unfortunately, conditions in those institutions were still deplorable—children were often restrained in handcuffs and leg irons—and by the mid-1800's, efforts were made to reform the facilities. Following their incarceration, juvenile offenders were often released into apprenticeships and forced to learn a trade.

Accompanying the reform movement was an effort to find and understand the root cause of delinquent behavior. Prevention and reformation were emphasized instead of mere punishment. Poverty and urbanization were seen as major causes of delinquency. In response, juvenile institutions which provided formal training for delinquent children—known as reform schools—were founded, and many troubled children were sent westward to rural areas to live and work on farms.

At the turn of the century, there were efforts to form a juvenile justice system separate from the adult criminal justice system. The idea behind establishing a juvenile court was to bring all children under the supervision of the state, which was given the role of surrogate parent ("parens patriae"), entrusting it with the job of determining the cause of juvenile misbehavior and prescribing appropriate rehabilitative treatment.

In 1899, the first juvenile court was established in Chicago, and by 1945, there was a juvenile court established in every state, each with its own set of laws concerning the handling of children who find their way into the system. Thus, America has no uniform juvenile justice system. Rather, it has 51 separate systems—each with its own history, its own balance of powers, and its own laws, policies, practices, and approaches to handling juvenile crime. Therefore, the reader is advised to check the law of his or her own jurisdiction when confronted with a specific problem.

OVERVIEW OF THE MODERN DAY JUVENILE JUSTICE SYSTEM

Classification of Juveniles

The objectives of the juvenile justice system are to deter children from becoming criminals and to protect children who are unable to protect themselves. Children who come in contact with the juvenile justice system generally fall into one or more of three categories: the delinquent child; the status offender, and the abused or neglected child.

The Delinquent Child

The delinquent child is one who commits criminal acts, but who receives more lenient treatment due to his or her minority. The trend has turned more towards rehabilitation rather than punishment, in an effort to save these children before they are able to turn into adult criminals.

The Status Offender

The juvenile status offender is one who commits acts which are not criminal in nature, but which nevertheless require some sort of intervention and disciplinary attention merely because of the age of the offender—his or her "status." Examples of status offenders are runaways, truants and children whose parents are unable to control and discipline them. In some jurisdictions, such status offenders are placed in special categories, such as persons in need of "supervision" (PINS), while in other jurisdictions, status offenders are still placed under the general heading of "delinquents."

The Abused or Neglected Child

Many children require protection by the juvenile authorities because they have been neglected or abused by their caretaker, usually a parent or legal guardian. The manner in which these children are handled by the juvenile court is explored in more detail elsewhere in this almanac.

The Three Branches of the System

The police department, the juvenile court, and the juvenile corrections unit are the three components of the juvenile justice system with which a child may come in contact.

Four stages make up the juvenile justice process: custody, intake, adjudication and disposition. The first step, custody, refers to the detention of the child by law enforcement authorities—i.e., the police; the intake process is carried out by the intake probation officer; the adjudication process, where a child may or may not be adjudicated delinquent, is carried out by the judge through a hearing; and the disposition, similar to sentencing in a criminal trial, is made by the judge, usually after consideration of probation department reports. Children who enter the system do not necessarily go through all of those stages, and depending on the circumstances, may be released prior to the final disposition stage.

POLICE AND THE JUVENILE

The police are the first to come in contact with the juvenile offender. Today, most police departments have established special units within the department to reach out to children and attempt to deter delinquent behavior. When juvenile misconduct is detected, the police are empowered to investigate and take appropriate action against the offenders, which may include taking the child into custody—tantamount to an arrest—depending on the facts.

Most state statutes allow the police to take a child into custody with or without a court order, depending on the circumstances. A child may be taken into custody without a court order if the police have reasonable grounds to do so, for example, if they have reason to believe that the child has committed a delinquent act or that the child is a status offender, such as a runaway or a truant, whose actions would not be punishable but for the child's minority.

Nevertheless, case law has held that the police cannot stop and search a child out of curiosity or on a mere hunch. In order to justify a stop and search, the police officer must have reasonable suspicion that wrongdoing has occurred and the person to be stopped was somehow involved in that wrongdoing. In addition, the police officer must be able to articulate the specific facts upon which this suspicion is based.

For example, if a police officer comes across a child "hanging out" in the mall, in the morning on a day when school is in session, the police officer

THE JUVENILE JUSTICE SYSTEM

may reasonably believe that the child is a truant. Based on that reasonable belief, the police officer is justified in stopping the child to ascertain the child's age and identity. However, if it were a holiday or after school hours, the police officer would have no right to stop and question the child, even if the officer had a gut feeling that the child was involved in some misbehavior.

The police officer can usually exercise various options when dealing with juvenile misconduct and may choose to handle a particular situation informally, e.g., by notifying the child's parents or by giving the child a "second chance." This is often the outcome when the police are confronted with a status offender.

When a particular juvenile offense is serious enough, the police officer may take the more formal action of taking the child into custody pending an investigation, and if it appears that detention is necessary, referring the child to the juvenile court. Accordingly, police officers have great discretion in handling the children with whom they come in contact, not all of whom can be considered delinquents.

When the police are confronted with a serious delinquent act, which results in taking the child into custody, they must abide by the special rules set up to protect the rights of children in custody. Those rights are discussed in more detail elsewhere in this almanac. Foremost, the police cannot question a child in the same manner as they would question an adult. Many factors are taken into account to determine whether any statements made during questioning may be used against the child, even if those statements were given voluntarily and the child was read the Miranda rights. Examples of such factors are the age and maturity of the child, the duration of questioning, and the presence of the parents.

In addition to dealing with juvenile misconduct, the police also intervene in cases of child neglect and abuse. If the police receive a complaint that a child is being neglected or abused, they must investigate the allegation to determine if the child is in danger and in need of protection. Such complaints can range from a child who has been left alone to a child who has been severely battered. If after careful consideration, a determination is made that the child is in danger, the police may remove the child from the home and place the child with the social services agency designated to handle such cases. Depending on the situation, the parental figure may be taken into custody or may receive a warning, and the police may refer the case to the social services department for further recommendations. The topic of child abuse and neglect is discussed in more detail elsewhere in this almanac.

In summary, the police are usually the first of the three units of the juvenile justice system to come in contact with the juvenile offender. The manner in which the police officer decides to dispose of a particular situation depends in large part upon the seriousness of the particular act of misconduct and the past history of the child. The police officer's wide discretion in handling a particular situation can mean the child will get off with a "slap on the wrist" or the child will continue through the various levels of the juvenile court system until his or her delinquent act is finally adjudicated and a disposition is made.

THE JUVENILE COURT

The juvenile court, also known as the family court in some jurisdictions, was established to handle cases involving children up to a statutorily defined age. The majority of states have designated age 18 as the upper limit, although some states limit jurisdiction to age 16 and other states extend juvenile court jurisdiction over children up to the age of 21.

The juvenile court may play many roles depending on the type of case it hears. It generally deals with situations involving delinquent, wayward, and neglected and abused children. For example, the juvenile court serves to protect society by rehabilitating and punishing delinquent youth; trying to change the path of wayward youth, such as truants and runaways; and attempting to protect neglected and abused children from their abusers, and punish the guilty parties.

The Delinquent Child

When a child is referred to the juvenile court, usually by the police, but sometimes by parents or school officials, the first stage they encounter is the intake process, carried out by the juvenile probation system, which is generally governed by the juvenile court. During this stage, the intake probation officer reviews the case to determine whether the child is in the proper jurisdiction and whether the facts of the case, and the background of the child, warrant a formal hearing, in which case a delinquency petition is filed.

Alternatively, the child may be referred out of the system for informal handling and treatment, usually by social services agencies, or placed on some type of informal probation. The children remaining in the system then move on to the next stage, which is the adjudicatory hearing, carried out before the juvenile court judge.

The purpose of the adjudicatory hearing is to determine whether the child is delinquent. The juvenile court judge, like the police officer, has a great deal of discretion in handling the juveniles who come before the court. The judge can determine that the child is delinquent, based on the testimony and evidence presented during the hearing. He or she can also refer the child out of the system to various social service agencies, place the child on probation without a finding of delinquency, or dismiss the case altogether.

In addition, as further discussed below, the judge can seek transfer of a delinquency case to an adult criminal court and in some states, the juvenile court is bypassed and the adult criminal court is automatically given jurisdiction over certain crimes.

Once it is determined that the child is delinquent, the child proceeds to the next and final stage in the juvenile court process—the disposition hearing, which is similar to a sentencing hearing in adult criminal court. To determine an appropriate disposition for the delinquent child, the judge considers the presentencing investigation report prepared by the juvenile probation officer, which sets forth the child's background and contains a disposition recommendation for the judge. Based on the report and recommendation, the judge comes up with an appropriate punishment, which can range anywhere from a simple scolding, to restitution, to incarceration in a juvenile correctional facility.

The Status Offender

Many states attempt to separate the delinquent child from the status offender," (also referred to as "PINS," "CHINS," or "MINS," that is Person, Child or Minor in Need of Supervision, depending on the jurisdiction). Although status offenses, such as disobedience, running away, or truancy, are not crimes, the court intervenes in such misbehavior to avoid its escalation into criminal behavior. Children who have committed status offenses are usually given more informal hearings than delinquent children.

The Neglected or Abused Child

The juvenile court has jurisdiction over the protection of children who are suspected to be neglected or abused. Although these cases are handled much more informally than delinquency cases, there are certain procedural requirements. For example, parents who are suspected of neglecting or abusing their child have the right to an attorney and must be given adequate notice. Evidence must be presented at the hearing which proves the allegations.

Since the well-being of a child is at stake, however, the standard of proof used by the juvenile court is much lower than the criminal "beyond a reasonable doubt" standard. For example, many juvenile courts utilize the "preponderance of the evidence" standard. There is a trend towards diverting neglect and abuse cases from the juvenile court system to the social services agencies, since such cases often stem from family problems likely to require treatment and counseling.

TRANSFER FROM JUVENILE COURT TO ADULT CRIMINAL COURT

The trend among the states has been to make it easier for juvenile offenders to be treated as adults. The categories of offenses for which transfer is appropriate has been expanded and the minimum age limits have been lowered. In addition, more restrictions have been placed on the court's discretion in transfer and prosecutors have been given greater authority over transfer decisions. In addition, many states have enacted legislation which requires automatic transfer to adult criminal court in cases involving serious or violent offenses and/or repeat offenders. In fact, all states now allow adult criminal prosecution of juveniles in certain circumstances.

A table of state minimum and maximum ages for original juvenile court jurisdiction in delinquency cases is set forth in Appendix 1.

Judicial Waiver

The most common method for transferring jurisdiction over juveniles from juvenile court to adult criminal court is judicial waiver. Forty-seven states authorize or require juvenile court judges to waive jurisdiction over individual cases involving minors and allow prosecution in adult criminal courts. Waiver provisions differ among the states in the degree of decision-making flexibility the court is allowed to exercise.

A list of states with judicial waiver provisions is set forth in Appendix 2.

Discretionary Waiver

In forty-six states, the waiver decision is completely within the discretion of the judge thus he or she is not required to transfer an otherwise appropriate case to the adult criminal court. In most of these states, there are certain criteria which must be met before the court can exercise the discretion to transfer the case to adult criminal court. For example, the minor must meet a minimum age requirement, the offense charged must be of a certain type, and the minor must have a significant prior record of offenses.

In addition, due process requires that the court hold a hearing in which evidence may be presented on behalf of the juvenile directed at the waiver issue. In order to proceed with transfer, the court must find that the minor is no longer amenable to treatment as a juvenile. The prosecution seeking to transfer the case to adult criminal court bears the burden of proof in the hearing. Generally, the standard of proof is by a preponderance of the evidence, however, six states require a higher standard, i.e., by clear and convincing evidence.

If the prosecution is successful in having the juvenile's case transferred to criminal court, six states provide that the criminal court may exercise jurisdiction over the offense that triggered the waiver as well as any lesser included offenses. In nine states, the criminal court is authorized jurisdiction over any offense which arose out of the same course of conduct as the waived offense, and one state gives the criminal court jurisdiction over all offenses involving the juvenile.

Presumptive Waiver

In sixteen states, there is a rebuttable presumption in favor of waiver in certain types of cases. The statutory criteria triggering waiver varies among the states. In some states, the seriousness of the offense — e.g., a violent felony—is the most important factor regardless of the child's age. In other states, it is the age of the child that matters even if the offense is less serious.

The juvenile who meets the statutory criteria for transfer bears the burden of proving that the case should not be removed to adult criminal court. Five of those states require the juvenile to meet the higher standard of proof that transfer is unjustified — i.e., by clear and convincing evidence.

Mandatory Waiver

In fifteen states, waiver is mandatory in cases that meet certain statutory criteria including age and level of offense. In these states, the proceedings are begun in juvenile court for the purpose of determining whether the statutory criteria for transfer have been met. If so, the case is transferred to adult criminal court.

Prosecutorial Discretion

In sixteen states, prosecutors have discretion over whether to directly file a certain case involving a minor in juvenile or criminal court. In those states, both the juvenile court and the adult criminal court have jurisdiction to hear the case regardless of the juvenile's age, record or the type of offense committed, however, the prosecutor makes the determination as to where to file the case and such determination is generally not reviewable. A minority of those states require the prosecutor to weigh certain factors in making their decision, such as age and level of offense.

A list of states with prosecutorial discretion provisions is set forth in Appendix 3.

Statutory Exclusion

In twenty-nine states, certain types of cases are excluded by statute from the jurisdiction of the juvenile court and adult criminal court jurisdiction is required. These cases generally involve serious, violent offenses, and/or offenders with a significant history of such offenses. The states which exercise statutory exclusion are in addition to the states that mandate waiver of certain categories of juvenile offenders to criminal court, as set forth above. Thus, in 38 states, jurisdiction is given to the adult criminal court over juvenile offenders either by mandatory waiver, statutory exclusion, or under both provisions.

In those states which exercise statutory exclusion, the statutory definition of a delinquent child generally excludes any person charged with a certain offense, are of a certain age, and/or who have a significant prior record. In such cases, the juvenile is charged and tried in adult criminal court as if her or she were an adult. In some states, it is only the most serious types of offenses which trigger this statutory exclusion, such as first degree murder.

A list of states with statutory exclusion provisions is set forth in Appendix 4.

Minimum Age Provisions for Transfer

Twenty-three states have at least one provision for transferring juveniles to criminal court for which no minimum age is specified although other statutory provisions may provide for a minimum age below which a child cannot even be charged with criminal responsibility. In the rest of the states, minimum ages generally range from 10 to 15 years old.

A list of states with minimum age provisions is set forth in Appendix 5.

Reverse Waiver Provisions

In 24 states, a juvenile who is being prosecuted in adult criminal court may petition to have the case transferred to juvenile court for adjudication or disposition. In these states, where a juvenile case is begun in adult criminal court either by a prosecutorial direct file provision or a statutory exclusion provision, the criminal court has the opportunity to consider whether adult prosecution is appropriate in the particular case. The adult criminal court may use the same type of inquiries made by a juvenile court in waiving jurisdiction, e.g., best interests of the child.

A list of states with reverse waiver provisions is set forth in Appendix 6.

Automatic Transfer Provisions

Thirty-four states have enacted provisions which provide that juveniles who have previously been prosecuted as adults will be tried as an adult for any subsequent offenses. These provisions are generally referred to as "once an adult/always an adult" provisions. In those states, a subsequent offense generally triggers either an automatic waiver provision or a statutory exclusion provision. In almost all of those states, except California, Delaware, Idaho and Mississippi, conviction of the original offense is required. In some states, this provision is only triggered depending on the juvenile's age or the seriousness of the subsequent offense.

A list of states with automatic transfer provisions is set forth in Appendix 7.

Transfer Provisions for Nonviolent Offenders

Although transfer of juveniles from juvenile court to adult criminal court is generally intended for serious, violent offenses, a number of states allow or require adult criminal prosecution of nonviolent offenses as well. For example, nineteen states authorize or mandate adult criminal court prosecution of juveniles who are accused of drug offenses. If the juvenile is over a certain age, twenty states permit waivers for any criminal offense and nineteen states allow or require adult prosecution for any felony. Twenty-one states require or allow adult prosecution of juveniles accused of certain property offenses such as arson or burglary and eleven states authorize or mandate adult prosecution of certain offenses which are not necessarily considered violent, such as escape, soliciting a minor to join a gang, aggravated driving under the influence, auto theft, perjury, and treason.

A list of states with transfer provisions for nonviolent offenders is set forth in Appendix 8.

THE EVOLUTION OF JUVENILE RIGHTS

Because the juvenile court was mainly established to assist children through rehabilitation, rather than to inflict punishment, many of the legal rights afforded adults subject to criminal prosecution, such as the right to an attorney, were initially waived in juvenile court. The intention was to deal with delinquent children informally without subjecting them to the formalities of a trial. However, this led to abuse of the child's rights—rights which the system did not recognize.

In 1967, a landmark decision in *In re Gault* was handed down by the Supreme Court. The Court held that the rights guaranteed under the United States Constitution applied to children as well as adults. The 15-year-old plaintiff in that case, Gerald Gault, was committed to a juvenile detention facility until the age of 21 because he was found guilty of making an obscene phone call to a neighbor. Such a crime, if committed by an adult, would probably have resulted in a fine or small jail sentence.

At that time, children's basic constitutional rights were not recognized. During the proceedings which led up to Gault's commitment, neither the child nor his parents were given notice of the charges; the child was not given the opportunity to be represented by an attorney; the neighbor was not required to testify or undergo questioning concerning the incidet; there was no written record of the legal proceeding; and the child had no right to appeal the court's decision.

In its defense, the state argued that a juvenile proceeding should be carried out informally, and with secrecy, to protect the child's reputation. However, the U.S. Supreme Court disagreed, holding that in situations where a child is in danger of losing his or her freedom, the child's rights should parallel those of the adult counterpart. The Court held that the following constitutional rights apply to children:

1. The right to notice of the charges leveled against the child.

2. The right to be represented by an attorney.

3. The right to confront his or her accusers, and to cross-examine witnesses who testify against the child.

4. The right to be informed of his or her Fifth Amendment Miranda right not to make statements which may be incriminating.

5. The right to a written record of the proceedings, which is particularly important should the child decide to appeal the juvenile court judge's decision.

Following the Gault decision, the Supreme Court handed down additional decisions concerning the rights of children, such as the reasonable doubt standard of proof, and the right not to be retried for the same offense twice—i.e., double jeopardy.

CONFIDENTIALITY OF JUVENILE COURT PROCEEDINGS

Traditionally, juvenile court proceedings were closed to the public and the juvenile offender's name and records remained confidential. The reasoning for nondisclosure was to protect the juvenile from suffering a lifelong stigma from wrongs committed during youth. However, as juvenile crime has become more serious and violent, the trend among the states has been to place limits on these confidentiality provisions, and to open juvenile court proceedings to the public where the offense is particularly serious or violent.

Presently, thirty states open juvenile court proceedings to the public where the offense charged is serious or violent and/or the juvenile is a repeat offender. Following this trend, limitations have also been placed on the confidentiality of the juvenile's name and record where the offense was particularly serious or violent.

A chart summarizing state limitations on confidentiality of juvenile court proceedings and records for serious and violent juvenile offenders is set forth at Appendix 9.

THE PROCESS OF JUVENILE CORRECTIONS

Placement in a Juvenile Correctional Facility

A child who is adjudicated delinquent may be committed to a juvenile correction facility. The stated goal of such a facility is to rehabilitate the delinquent child and return him or her into society as a productive member. The intent is also to protect the community from the misdeeds of the delinquent and to punish the child.

The profile of a typical child confined in a juvenile correctional facility is a minority male child, 15 years of age, from a lower social class, who has had prior contact with the juvenile court system. Many of the children are status offenders. This is particularly true of the female child, who is confined more often than her male counterpart for similar offenses.

A table demonstrating the juvenile justice population by age and gender is set forth at Appendix 10.

Generally, there are two types of correctional facilities in which children who have been adjudicated delinquent are placed: the non-secure and the secure. The non-secure facility, also known as a training school, usually offers the child an education or occupational training, and provides guidance and counseling in a structured environment. Although the children placed in a non-secure facility require removal from society, they are not deemed a serious risk to society.

The secure facilities generally house children who have committed the most serious offenses, and have a history of delinquent behavior. The secure facility is a controlled and restrictive environment, usually enclosed by security devices which prohibit movement in and out of the facility.

The Rights of Juveniles in Correctional Facilities

Children who have been committed to state-run juvenile correctional facilities maintain certain rights during their commitment. Children are entitled to receive proper health care, nourishment, clothing, and basically decent living quarters during their incarceration. They are entitled to communicate with family and friends, in person and by mail and telephone. They are entitled to confer with their attorney.

The institution must maintain a safe environment for the child. For example, children are generally classified according to the offenses committed. Children who have committed acts of violence must be separated from children who have committed nonviolent acts. In addition, the institution is responsible for the acts of its employees, and must properly train and supervise those employees or risk liability.

Since the juvenile justice system is concerned primarily with the treatment and rehabilitation of the juvenile offender, the institution must provide the child with an adequate education plan. When discipline is necessary, however, it can not be imposed until the child has exercised his or her rights, such as the right to receive notice of the offense, and the right to present his or her case at a hearing before an impartial hearing examiner. The hearing examiner's decision, which must be in writing, can be appealed by the child. In any event, the disciplinary measure cannot involve cruel and unusual punishment.

Blended Sentencing

Due to the increase in serious and violent crime among juveniles, twenty-two states have enacted blended sentencing legislation. Blended sentencing gives the court the choice of punishing serious juvenile offenders with juvenile or adult correctional sanctions rather than restricting them to one system.

A list of states with blended sentencing provisions for serious juvenile offenders is set forth in Appendix 11.

RESTORATIVE JUSTICE AND VICTIMS OF JUVENILE CRIME

The trend among juvenile courts is recognition that the juvenile offender owes an obligation to his or her victim and the community in which the offense took place. The juvenile justice system is also recognizing that victims of juvenile crime also have the right to be active participants in the justice process just as occurs in the adult criminal justice system. Traditionally, victims of juvenile offenders have had far fewer rights than victims of adult offenders, in large part due to the historically closed and confidential nature of juvenile proceedings.

Most states have passed laws recognizing the rights of victims of juvenile crime. Some of those states limit the rights to victims of juveniles whose offenses would be felonies if committed by adults and others have not imposed such a limit. Almost half of the states have a fairly comprehensive list of rights for victims of serious juvenile offenses.

Most of this legislation focuses on three primary areas:

1. Disclosure of information about the offender and his or her family;

2. Defining victims rights; and

3. Opening hearings to victims and giving them the right to attend all juvenile proceedings.

Additional provisions that seek to compensate the victim and/or include the victim in the juvenile justice process include:

1. Notification of hearings or the offenders' release from custody;

2. A victims bill of rights for juvenile crime victims or inclusion under an existing victims bill of rights;

3. The right to submit a victim impact statement;

4. A victims bureau for dispensing services to victims;

5. The right to restitution either by the juvenile or the juvenile's parents; and

6. The right to confidentiality of the victim's address.

CAPITAL PUNISHMENT AND THE JUVENILE

In General

Up until 1988, sentencing a child to death for commission of a capital crime, such as murder, was legal in approximately 25 states. However, in *Thompson v. Oklahoma,* the Supreme Court intervened in the execution of a 15-year-old boy, convicted of brutally murdering his brother-in-law. The Court held that the age of 15 was too young to die, and that states which have the death penalty must establish a minimum age for executions. In effect, since the court established that 15 was too young, it effectively set 16 as the minimum age. In 1989, the Court upheld the death penalty for those who were 16 or 17 when they committed the crime.

Presently, sixteen states permit the death penalty for offenders who are younger than 18 years of age. In 14 states, the death penalty may not be imposed unless the offender is 18 or older. The federal government also specifies age 18 as the minimum age for a death penalty sentence. Eight states do not specify any minimum age, although the *Thompson* decision effectively bars the execution of a child under the age of 16.

Current Prisoners under Juvenile Death Sentences

As of December 31, 1997, 67 persons—all male—were under sentence of death in 12 different states in connection with their convictions for juvenile crimes. Their number constitutes approximately two percent of the total death row population of 3,400. All of the prisoners were convicted and sentenced to death for murder. The majority of victims were reportedly White adults, half of whom were female.

All of the condemned were either 16 or 17 at the time they committed the crime. Their ages now range between 18 and 39. Their time spent on death row ranges from several weeks to almost 20 years. Twenty-six of the juvenile offenders under sentence of death are in Texas, the largest number held in any one state's death row.

Although the total number of prisoners under sentence of death has increased almost 200% since 1983, the number of juvenile offenders on death row has not risen quite as rapidly. In 1983, there were 33 juvenile offenders under sentence of death compared to 67 today. This is attributed to the fact that the number of new juvenile death sentences each year is relatively equal to the number of death sentence reversals combined with executions.

CHAPTER 2:
JUVENILE VIOLENCE

IN GENERAL

America is a violent society. All one needs to do is turn on the evening news to validate that statement. Stories of murder, rape, and other violent acts are presented in all of their gory details, and are no longer sensational because they have become all too common. It appears that people have become desensitized to the violence—it is just too much to handle. The statistics are alarming—in 1989, 21,500 people were murdered in the U.S.A. Violence in America far surpasses any other industrialized nation. In fact, some foreign embassies have issued safety warnings to their citizens planning to visit America.

It is a sad fact that much of the violence in America is committed by juveniles. It is no longer uncommon to hear stories of murder and rape where the perpetrators have barely entered their teens. Indeed, violence among children much younger—as young as age 7—is also becoming more prevalent.

THE CAUSES OF VIOLENCE

Physiological Causes

Studies have shown that many violent criminals suffer some degree of neurological damage. In fact, there appears to be a correlation between the degree of violence and the severity of neurological impairment. In addition, some experts also believe that childhood aggression—often a precursor to violence—may be genetically or hormonally based, particularly in boys.

Sociological Causes

The Abusive Family

Children often learn violence at a very young age by watching their parents—their very first role models—and tend to imitate what they witness. Family violence, such as child abuse and spousal abuse, is epidemic in this country. The rejection an abused child generally feels, often results in poor self-esteem, which is a breeding ground for anger and aggressive behavior. Statistically, the violent criminal—male and female—is likely to have been brought up in an abusive environment. In addition, the prevalence of the single-female-parent family, where boys are deprived of strong male role models, causes many adolescent males to look outside of the home for a replacement. Unfortunately, more often than not, their replacement role model is the neighborhood pimp, drug dealer, or gang.

The topic of child abuse and neglect is discussed more fully in Chapter 4 of this almanac.

The Role of Peer Pressure

When support and encouragement is lacking in the family structure, children are more apt to turn to their friends for approval. In fact, research has shown that the motivation behind a child joining a gang is the need to belong and to be recognized. The period of childhood through adolescence is a time of learning for all children. Without proper guidance by their adult role models, children are left to experiment on their own, their only feedback coming from their also inexperienced peers.

Much delinquent behavior is committed by children while they are with their peers. This may account for much of the gang violence that is becoming more commonplace, particularly in large urban areas, although gangs are springing up all over the country. The formation of gangs among teenagers is certainly not a new phenomenon, but the nature of the gang has changed considerably. In the 1950s, the weapons of choice were fists, chains, and knives, and the children did not have access to large sums of money. That has changed, in large part due to the involvement of gangs in the profitable business of drug distribution and the availability of sophisticated weapons, which they do not hesitate to use if their operations are threatened.

The Influence of Television and Other Media

Television—"America's favorite babysitter"—plays both a positive and negative role in the socialization of children. With remote control in hand, children can readily flip through the channels and view programs ranging from educational television, where they first learn their ABC's, to programs which depict the most deviant, violent, and immoral behavior one can imagine. Unlike the movies, where admission is controlled by age, television is basically uncontrollable without continuous parental supervision. Never before have young children been exposed to such violence on screen.

Children learn how to behave in a socially acceptable manner by studying the behavior of their parents, and other role models, and copying those actions. In this connection, studies have found that children who are frequently exposed to violence on television exhibit more aggressive behavior and become more accepting of violence as a means of solving their own problems.

In addition, there is a positive correlation between television violence and actual violence. In fact, "television intoxication" has been used as a defense in cases where children have been arrested for particularly violent offenses, after viewing programs which contained similar story lines. With the advent of cable television, and the stretching of the permissible boundaries of regular television, one can only conclude that this trend will continue.

Other Influences

In addition to television violence, many of the popular video games enjoyed by young children involve an alarming amount of violence, and it appears that so-called war toys are more popular now than ever. Children are also exposed to violence through the music they listen to which, in some cases, has been linked to teenage suicide and murder.

VIOLENCE IN THE SCHOOL

Another area of concern is the astronomical incidence of violence occurring in the nation's schools. The nature of the violence is even more alarming. School officials are not just breaking up fistfights any more. They are confiscating drugs and weapons, dodging bullets, and rushing critically injured children to emergency rooms.

Schools are no longer a safe haven where children are sent to learn and mature. In fact, many schools have become armed camps where children are no longer greeted at the door by their teachers, but are confronted by dogs who are trained to sniff them for drugs, and metal detectors designed to expose illegal weapons. The statistics concerning school violence are frightening. According to a 1988 study by the United States Department of Justice, approximately 500,000 acts of violence occurred at the high school level per month.

Violence has become an expected part of the school day. Robberies, shootings, and other physical attacks are common in many schools, particularly in large urban areas. Children are afraid to go to school for fear that they will be killed, in large part due to the accessibility of guns to young people. Otherwise peaceful students have resorted to carrying illegal handguns for the sole purpose of self-defense.

Recent Statistics

According to the Bureau of Justice Statistics, from July 1, 1997 through June 30, 1998, there were 60 school-associated violent deaths in the United States. Forty-seven of these violent deaths were homicides, 12 were suicides, and one was a teenager killed by a law enforcement officer in the line of duty. Thirty-five of the 47 school-associated homicides were of school age children. Seven of the 12 school-associated suicides were of school age children.

The percentage of students in grades 9 through 12 who have been threatened or injured with a weapon on school property has not changed significantly in recent years. In 1993, 1995, and 1997, about 7 to 8 percent of students reported being threatened or injured with a weapon such as a gun, knife, or club on school property in the past 12 months.

In 1998, 12- through 18-year-old students living in urban, suburban, and rural locales were equally vulnerable to serious violent crime and theft at school. Away from school, urban and suburban students were more vulnerable to serious violent crime and theft than were rural students

Younger students ages 12 through 14 were more likely than older students ages 15 through 18 to be victims of crime at school. Males were more likely than females to report being threatened or injured with a weapon on school property.

In 1996-97, 10 percent of all public schools reported at least one serious violent crime to the police or a law enforcement representative.

Principals' reports of serious violent crimes included murder, rape or other type of sexual battery, suicide, physical attack or fight with a weapon, or robbery. Another 47 percent of public schools reported a less serious violent or nonviolent crime. Crimes in this category include physical attack or fight without a weapon, theft/larceny, and vandalism. The remaining 43 percent of public schools did not report any of these crimes to the police.

In 1999, public school students were more likely to report having been victims of violent crime during the previous 6 months than were private school students. However, public school students were equally as private school students to experience theft.

Elementary schools were much less likely than either middle or high schools to report any type of crime in 1996-97. They were much more likely to report vandalism than any other crime. At the middle and high school levels, physical attack or fight without a weapon was generally the most commonly reported crime in 1996-97. Theft or larceny was more common at the high school than at the middle school level.

Nevertheless, the studies also show that students are more likely to be victims of serious violent crime away from school than at school. From July 1, 1997 through June 30, 1998, a total of 2,752 children ages 5 through 19 were victims of homicide in the United States. During this same time period, students ages 12 through 18 were more likely to be victims of nonfatal serious violent crime—including rape, sexual assault, robbery, and aggravated assault—away from school than when they were at school. In 1998, approximately 550,000 students in this age range were victims of such crimes away from schools, compared with about 253,000 at school.

In 1998, students in this age range were also victims to about 1.2 million nonfatal violent crimes at school compared to about 1.3 million away from school. As for non-violent crimes, such as theft, students ages 12 through 18 were more likely to be victims at school than away from school. In 1998, about 1.6 million thefts occurred at school compared to about 1.2 million away from school.

Violence Against Teachers

Although most violence occurs among students, the statistics concerning violence against teachers are alarming. According to recent figures, approximately 5,000 high school teachers are physically attacked each month, and approximately 100,000 teachers are verbally abused and/or threatened with physical violence.

Over the 5-year period from 1994 through 1998, teachers were victims of 1,755,000 non-fatal crimes at school, including 1,087,000 thefts and 668,000 violent crimes, i.e. rape or sexual assault, robbery, and aggravated and simple assault. In the same period, senior high school and middle/junior high school teachers were more likely to be victims of violent crimes than elementary school teachers.

Although criminal prosecution is carried out against perpetrators of physical violence—students and parents—the Supreme Court cited the First Amendment in striking down an attempt by several states to criminalize verbal abuse against a teacher on school premises.

Zero Tolerance Policies

According to the National Center for Education Statistics (NCES), three-quarters or more of all schools reported having zero tolerance policies for various student offenses. About 90 percent of schools reported zero tolerance policies for firearms (94 percent) and weapons other than firearms (91 percent). Eighty-seven and 88 percent had policies of zero tolerance for alcohol and drugs, respectively. Seventy-nine percent had a zero tolerance policy for violence and 79 percent had a zero tolerance policy for tobacco. Schools with no crime reported were less likely to have a zero tolerance policy for violence (74 percent) than schools that had reported one or more serious crimes (85 percent).

TEENAGE SUICIDE

Adolescent suicide has more than quadrupled since 1950, and the rate of suicide is escalating. It is the leading cause of death among teenagers. Nevertheless, experts have suggested that the incidence of adolescent suicide is understated. They believe that many teenage deaths deemed accidental are actually intentional, such as drug overdoses and automobile accidents.

Causation

The teenage years can be a difficult time for children, as they experience the rapid and unpredictable physical and emotional changes that accompany the onset of puberty. Teenagers tend to be insecure about their developing bodies, their sexual impulses, and the physical, emotional, and intellectual transition from childhood to adolescence. In addition to those changes, many children are forced to deal with such stressful situations, such as scholastic and peer pressures, divorcing parents, and the death of loved ones.

When parents divorce, a child's life is often turned upside down. The child's emotions may be overlooked as the parents concentrate on their feud. The child may feel confused, hurt and angry, but he or she may be afraid to express those feelings for fear of choosing sides between the parents he or she loves. Sometimes a child harbors guilt, believing to be somehow responsible for the breakup. The child does not know where to direct this anger and hurt, and often becomes depressed.

According to the experts, depression is the primary cause of adolescent suicide. Although childhood is generally viewed as the "carefree years," it is a sad fact that children can and do become depressed and lonely. Many children who attempt suicide suffer from low self-esteem and a sense of hopelessness. Suicide, not unlike teenage alcohol and drug use, is their way of escaping what seems to them to be a world full of overwhelming problems. In that connection, studies have shown that teenagers who use alcohol or drugs are at greater risk of suicide. Depression may also be due to physiologically based problems. When depression has a biochemical basis, it can be treated with antidepressant drugs, usually prescribed during a course of therapy with a psychiatrist.

For some children, the underlying reason for a suicide attempt is not an actual desire to die, but a means of getting the attention they crave and the assurances that they are loved and needed. In fact, the majority of teenagers who attempt suicide do so in their own homes, during the time of day when they would most likely get caught, unlike older people who attempt suicide at night, when they are less likely to be discovered.

Statistics

According to the Bureau of Justice Statistics, from July 1, 1997 through June 30, 1998, 2,061 children ages 5 through 19 committed suicide. Girls are more likely to attempt suicide, but boys succeed more often. Children who live in rural areas are at a higher risk of suicide than their counterparts in the city. Native American teens are 10 times more likely to commit suicide than white teens. White teens are 5 more times likely to commit suicide than black teens. Even young children have committed suicide, although they possess much less understanding of the finality of the act than older children.

Warning Signs

There are numerous warning signs that may indicate that a child is at risk for suicide:

1. Depression—It is normal for teenagers to have their ups and downs, their good days and bad days. However, if a teenager is continuously in a depressed state, this is not normal.

2. Bad grades—This is particularly so if the child was previously a very good student and there has been a sudden unexplained drop in grades and a disinterest in school and the future.

3. Drug and/or alcohol abuse.

4. Threats of suicide—Threats of suicide should always be taken seriously because they are often cries for help.

5. Withdrawal from family, friends, and previous activities.

6. Decline in personal hygiene and appearance, and a change in sleeping and eating habits.

7. Preoccupation with death—This is sometimes represented by the music the child listens to, especially if it is a sudden departure from the child's usual preferences.

8. Preparation for death, such as making a will or parting with possessions.

CHAPTER 3:
ILLEGAL DRUGS AND ALCOHOL ABUSE

IN GENERAL

It is a fact that the United States has the highest percentage of teenage drug and alcohol use of any industrialized nation. Approximately one-half of all homicides, suicides, and fatal accidents, are reportedly associated with drug or alcohol use. Studies have also shown that drug use and crime are linked, and account for the increasing number of children who engage in criminal behavior, such as robbery, prostitution and drug dealing, to support their drug habits.

A directory of state agencies that assist substance abusers is set forth in Appendix 12.

TYPES OF ILLEGAL DRUGS USED BY CHILDREN

Substance abuse among children ranges from the use of the more accepted, legal drugs, such as alcohol and cigarettes, to the use of marijuana, inhalants—such as airplane glue and nitrous oxide, prescription drugs, hallucinogens—such as LSD, methamphetamine—such as ecstasy, and narcotics—such as heroin and cocaine.

Marijuana

Marijuana is derived from the leaves of the Indian hemp plant. The leaves are dried, chopped, rolled into cigarette form or placed in a pipe, and smoked. Marijuana enters the bloodstream and affects the brain and nervous system, causing a variety of effects, including reduced coordination and reflexes, and distorted thinking.

Inhalants

Inhalants are chemicals which emit fumes that are inhaled, causing intoxication, loss of coordination, distorted perception and hallucinations. Overuse can lead to convulsions, brain damage and death.

Hallucinogens

Hallucinogens are natural and man-made drugs which can be taken orally or injected. They affect the brain's chemistry, causing distorted thinking, hallucinations, anxiety attacks and suicidal urges.

Methamphetamine

Methamphetamine is a stimulant drug which is quickly metabolized to amphetamine. It is used in pill form, or in powdered form by snorting or injecting. Crystallized methamphetamine is inhaled by smoking and is a considerably more powerful form of the drug. Some of the effects of methamphetamine use include: increased heart rate, wakefulness, physical activity and decreased appetite. Methamphetamine use can cause irreversible damage to the brain, producing strokes and convulsions, which can lead to death. Ecstasy, a new trendy and popular drug among teenagers is a refined and processed form of methamphetamine.

Cocaine

Cocaine is a narcotic drug which usually comes in the form of a white powder that is sniffed or injected by the user. It is derived from the coca plant. Cocaine is both a local anesthetic and a stimulant causing the user to experience a localized numbing sensation, as well as stimulation of the nervous system. Cocaine is extremely addictive. Overuse can cause hallucinations, nasal cavity ulcers, depression and death.

Because teenagers are still growing and developing, they are more likely than adults to suffer from the serious physiological and psychological damage cocaine causes, and are much more likely to become addicted in a shorter period of time.

Crack

Crack—a purified form of cocaine—is a deadly and destructive narcotic that has become the illegal drug of choice for many of the nation's youth because it is relatively inexpensive and, since it is smoked, it is easy to use. Crack is known to be far more dangerous and addictive than any of its predecessors, including heroin, and has been found to produce psychotic and violent behavior.

In fact, crack is much more dangerous than powdered cocaine. Because it is smoked, crack immediately enters the bloodstream and reaches the brain in less than 10 seconds, while sniffing powdered cocaine can take up to 5 minutes to reach the brain. The speed in which crack reaches the brain can cause immediate death, usually due to a heart attack or stroke, no matter how healthy the user is. Although both drugs are addictive, crack addiction occurs sooner due to its immediate assault on the brain. In fact, some users have reportedly become addicted after smoking crack for the first time.

TEENAGE ALCOHOL ABUSE

Historical Overview

Until the late 19th century, there were no minimum age laws regarding the consumption of alcohol. In fact, prior to that time, the frequent use of alcohol was widespread and acceptable for all age groups. Entire families would visit their local taverns, where drinking and fellowship was commonplace. Any problems resulting from alcohol consumption was attributed to the person, and not to the drug.

In the early 1900s, the states began enacting laws which prohibited the sale of alcohol to children. However, these laws were not strictly enforced, nor were children prohibited from drinking. As society became more industrialized, and the local tavern became more of a haven for working men where prostitution and gambling were readily available, alcohol took on a different image. Alcohol abuse was seen as the cause for growing immorality, crime, and violence. A movement to completely prohibit the use of alcohol took hold and was in large part responsible for passage of the 18th constitutional amendment and the Volstead Act in 1919, which made alcohol illegal.

Federal prohibition of alcohol was unsuccessful. It was impossible to enforce adequately and resulted in illegal liquor production and distribution. As a result, in 1933, the 21st constitutional amendment was passed which repealed prohibition, and alcohol once again became legal. Nevertheless, concern over the effects of alcohol continued to be an issue, and strict minimum age drinking laws—usually set at age 21—were enacted by all of the states.

During the Vietnam War, large numbers of young men were drafted at the age of 18, and in 1971, the 26th constitutional amendment lowered the federal voting age to 18. It thus struck many as ironic that a child was considered old enough to go to war and to vote, but was not permitted to drink a beer. In response, the minimum drinking age was lowered in many states.

Statistics

According to some studies, over 90% of teenagers experiment with alcohol at some time. Studies have also found that children are beginning to drink at a much younger age, and that some children first try alcohol somewhere between the ages of 11 and 14.

A great deal of research has been done to determine why teenagers are compelled to drink. Teenage alcohol use is largely due to such factors as peer pressure, and the learned behavior of parental alcohol use. If their friends are drinking, they may also want to drink to fit in with the group. At an age when children are most awkward in social situations, alcohol eases the tension. Nevertheless, according to the Surgeon General, almost one-third of teenagers who drink do so when they are alone, and 40% use alcohol as an escape from their problems. In addition, many children are curious about alcohol and its effects, and may want to imitate others they have seen drink.

Studies have shown that much of the violent crime that occurs is committed by individuals who are under the influence of alcohol. Children who drink have been found to exhibit aggressive behavior and engage in a disproportionate number of fights. Almost one-third of teenage murder victims are intoxicated at the time of their death. In addition, twenty percent of teenage suicides are committed while the adolescent is under the influence of alcohol.

Teenage Drinking and Driving

For a long time, the legal age for purchasing alcohol was 21 years old in most of the United States. Then, in the 1960s and early 1970s, many states lowered their minimum purchasing ages to 18 or 19 years old.

According to the Insurance Institute for Highway Safety, the consequences of this action indicated an increase in the number of 15-20 year-olds involved in nighttime fatal crashes. Although some states raised their legal drinking ages to try to combat this problem, it was found that teenagers would cross state lines to drink legally. As a result, the incidence of fatal automobile accidents across state lines, due to teenage drinking, rose considerably.

As a result of this and other studies with similar findings, a number of states raised their minimum alcohol purchasing ages—in some states back to 21 years old and in other states to 19 or 20. Subsequent research indicated that states which raised their minimum legal alcohol purchasing age experienced a 13 percent reduction in nighttime driver fatal crash involvement involving teenagers.

In 1984, 23 states had minimum alcohol purchasing ages of 21 years old. Also in 1984, the Commission on Drunken Driving, formed by President Ronald Reagan, announced its recommendation that there be a uniform minimum drinking age set at 21, based on studies which indicated that raising the drinking age would result in fewer teenage road fatalities. Since states set their own minimum drinking ages, the "carrot and the stick" approach—a fund-based method of coercion—had to be used to bring all 50 states into compliance with this recommendation.

Congress amended its Surface Transportation Bill—a source of federal funds available to the states for building roads—to provide that all states comply with its recommendation for a minimum drinking age of 21. Any state which did not comply within two years would lose a percentage of the funds allocated to that state. This threat of lost revenue worked, and by mid-1988, Federal legislation was enacted to withhold highway funds from the remaining 27 states if they did not follow suit. Since July 1988, all 50 states and the District of Columbia have required alcohol purchasers to be 21 years old.

Teenage drinking and driving—a deadly combination—continues to be a serious problem nevertheless. Alcohol is still readily available to the underage drinker, who does not have the necessary experience to handle either drinking or driving. Almost half of all teenagers who die in automobile accidents are drunk drivers, or are the passengers of a drunk teenage driver. In fact, alcohol-related automobile accidents are the primary cause of death in children between the ages of 15 and 24. In areas where the laws prohibiting drinking and driving are strictly enforced, however, the incidence of fatal automobile accidents is considerably lower.

Although young drivers are less likely than older teenagers and adults to drive after drinking alcohol, their crash risks are substantially higher when they do. This is especially true at low and moderate blood alcohol concentrations (BACs) and is thought to result from teenagers' relative inexperience with both drinking and driving.

Minimum alcohol purchasing age laws have been effective in reducing alcohol-related accidents involving teenagers, and many communities are strengthening enforcement of these laws. According to the National Highway Traffic Safety Administration, fatal crashes among young drivers declined dramatically as states adopted older purchasing ages, and by 1996 the statistic had declined to 24 percent, the biggest improvement for any age group.

Forty-seven states and the District of Columbia have established very low legal BAC thresholds for teenage drivers, and license suspension or another penalty may result from violations of these reduced blood alcohol concentration levels. Early research from states where this policy has been implemented—including states where zero is the legal alcohol limit for teenagers—indicates it might reduce teenagers' nighttime fatal crashes.

Federal legislation passed in 1995 encourages states to adopt and enforce "zero tolerance" or a 0.02 percent maximum BAC to combat alcohol-impaired driving among drivers younger than 21 years old. All but the Mississippi and Wisconsin laws apply to all drivers younger than 21 and impose a BAC threshold of 0.02 or less. Mississippi's threshold is 0.08, and the Wisconsin law applies to drivers younger than 19.

DRUG AND ALCOHOL ABUSE AND THE SCHOOL-AGE CHILD

According to the Bureau of Justice Statistics, there was an increase in the use of marijuana among students between 1993 and 1995, but no change between 1995 and 1997. In 1997, about 26 percent of ninth grade students had used marijuana in the last 30 days. Furthermore, in 1995 and 1997, almost one-third of all students in grades 9 through 12 reported that someone had offered, sold, or given them an illegal drug on school property. This was an increase from 1993 when 24 percent of such students reported that illegal drugs were available to them on school property.

In 1997, about 51 percent of students in grades 9 through 12 had at least one drink of alcohol in the previous 30 days. A much smaller percentage—about 6 percent—had at least one drink on school property during the same period.

CHAPTER 4:
CHILD ABUSE AND NEGLECT

HISTORICAL OVERVIEW

The maltreatment of children is not a modern day phenomena. Historically, children have endured beatings and other forms of severe physical cruelty at the hands of their parents, teachers and other caretakers. In fact, physical brutality was once seen as an acceptable form of punishment, known as "beating the devil out of the child."

Until the late 1800s, very little was done about child abuse, primarily because it was believed that children were the exclusive property of their parents, and the parent's right to discipline his or her children was unquestioned. In the late 19th century, attitudes began to change, and agencies were founded whose objectives were to prevent cruelty to children. Protection of children became a public responsibility, however, the problem remained hidden until the 1960s, when children's protective rights were recognized, reporting laws went into effect, and the magnitude of the problem was revealed.

CHILD NEGLECT

Improper Care

Child neglect occurs when a child is not properly cared for by his or her parents or legal guardian. Improper care may include the refusal or failure to provide the child with physical necessities, such as food, clothing, shelter, education, and medical or dental treatment; and the physical and/or emotional abandonment of the child.

It is important to stress that the behavior must be intentional to be deemed neglect. If the parent is financially unable to provide the child with such necessities, the family should be afforded social services, such as food stamps, medicaid, and other public assistance, as needed.

Physical Endangerment

Another form of neglect is physical endangerment, which may be found when a parent is so negligent in his or her supervision of the child that injury results. Parents are obligated to safeguard their children. Even though accidents can and do occur, if they are frequently due to the parent's inattentiveness, this may be considered physical endangerment neglect.

In addition, if a child is abandoned by a parent in a dangerous situation, whether or not physical injury resulted, this also constitutes physical endangerment. Of course, factors such as the child's age and maturity must necessarily be considered. For example, a preschooler is too young to be left alone in the home, no matter how mature he or she may seem to be.

Emotional Neglect

A child may be deemed emotionally neglected if his or her parent fails to provide appropriate nurturing and affection such that the child is in danger of developmental deficiency. For example, an infant who is never held, hugged or shown any affection may be considered neglected emotionally, as studies have shown that infants need physical stimulation in order to thrive.

Educational Neglect

Educational neglect occurs when a parent fails to enroll their child in school as required by the state's compulsory education statutes. In addition, if the parent permits a child to frequently skip school, this may also be deemed educational neglect. Educational neglect differs from truancy, which occurs when the child fails to attend school despite the parent's attempt to require attendance.

CHILD ABUSE

Physical Abuse

Physical abuse occurs when physical injury is inflicted upon, or permitted to be inflicted upon, a child, by his or her parent or legal guardian. Physical discipline by a parent is permitted in all states provided that it is reasonable and not excessive. Of course, no matter how difficult a child may act, a parent is never permitted to cause serious physical injury to the child. The "reasonableness" standard is largely dependent on the age of the child.

Emotional Abuse

Emotional abuse occurs when a child is subjected to treatment which endangers his or her psychological well-being. Again, discipline must be reasonable and not excessive. For example, grounding a disobedient child for a week may be considered reasonable, however, locking the child in a dark closet for an extended period of time would constitute emotional abuse. Emotional abuse may also occur in conjunction with physical abuse. For example, when a child is tortured by his or her parent, the mental scars may be more damaging and long-lasting than the physical scars.

CHILD SEXUAL ABUSE

In General

Child sexual abuse refers to the forced, tricked, or coerced sexual behavior between a young person and an older person. It includes rape, pedophilia, child prostitution and pornography, and incest. In recent years, there has been an attempt to recognize and deal with the problem of child sexual abuse, although the reported cases likely represent only a small fraction of the incidence of child sexual abuse. Since sexual abuse is a criminal offense, as well as a civil offense, investigations may be made by both child protective agencies and the police department.

Typical state penal laws prohibiting rape and sexual abuse are set forth in Appendix 13 and 14. A table setting forth the age criteria for statutory rape in each state is set forth in Appendix 15.

Intrafamilial Sexual Abuse

Children are always warned not to speak to strangers. Sadly, however, this admonition may not protect a child from becoming a victim of sexual abuse, because the abuser is most often a family member or close friend of the family—someone the child already trusts. This is how intrafamilial sexual abuse can persist in secrecy. Since the child has a trusting and loving relationship with the abuser, he or she may naively believe that the adult is acting appropriately. Alternatively, in many cases there are threats of retaliation if the child reveals the abuse, and the child submits out of fear.

PROFILE OF AN ABUSED OR NEGLECTED CHILD

Behavioral

Although one or more of the following behaviors may occasionally be found in a child who is not abused or neglected, they are behaviors which are often found in such children, and should not be overlooked:

1. Aggressiveness (extreme).

2. Anxiety.

3. Depression.

4. Fearfulness.

5. Hunger (habitual).

6. Immaturity.

7. Lack of Confidence.

8. Low self-esteem.

9. Self-hatred.

10. Sexual sophistication (beyond age level).

11. Withdrawal.

Physical

The physical indications of abuse or neglect are more readily discernible, and may include one or more of the following:

1. A habitually unkempt appearance.

2. Bruises, cuts, burns, welts, bites, etc., for which there is no reasonable explanation, particularly if there appears to be a continuing pattern of the same types of injuries.

3. Sexually transmitted disease.

4. Pregnancy.

MANDATORY REPORTING OF ABUSE AND NEGLECT

Every state has a statute which requires the reporting of known, as well as suspected, incidents of child abuse or neglect. Generally, professionals who come in contact with children are obligated to report suspected child abuse or neglect, or face criminal and civil penalties. They are referred to as mandatory reporters and include:

1. Medical or hospital personnel, such as doctors, dentists, nurses, and specialists.

2. Law enforcement personnel, such as police officers.

3. Social services personnel, such as social workers.

4. School personnel, such as teachers and guidance counselors.

5. Mental health professionals, such as psychiatrists and psychologists.

6. Child care providers.

All persons who suspect that a child is being abused or neglected may make a report to the appropriate authorities. In fact, in many states, ordinary citizens are also required by statute to report suspected child abuse or neglect.

In the past, people were concerned that they may be sued if they reported their suspicion of abuse or neglect, particularly if there was ultimately no finding of wrongdoing. In order to encourage persons to report suspected abuse and neglect, all states have enacted laws which provide that reporters are immune from civil or criminal liability as a result of the report, even if no finding of abuse or neglect was made, as long as the report was made in good faith.

This immunity applies even where there may have been a duty of confidentiality, such as accompanies the physician-patient relationship. Of course, if a report is made maliciously, and in bad faith, that person could be found liable.

CHILD ABUSE REPORTS

Abuse reports that are under investigation are generally recorded in a pending complaint file by the agency responsible for investigating such reports, such as the state's Department of Social Services. These reports typically include the names of both the child and the suspected abuser, their addresses, the type of abuse reported, the status of the investigations or legal proceedings, and whether a criminal investigation has been undertaken.

When the investigation is completed, the agency categorizes the report as unfounded, indicated, or founded. This labeling affects how the report is treated. An abuse report is unfounded when the agency decides that no substantial evidence exists that the alleged abuse occurred. It is possible, however, that the reported incident occurred but it does not reach the level of abuse. An unfounded report is generally removed from the pending complaint file as soon as possible and no record is kept of the report.

If the agency finds substantial evidence that abuse occurred, the report will be indicated. Indicated abuse reports are recorded in a statewide register. A report is founded when a court determines the evidence establishes abuse. This can happen in two ways. An agency that has determined that a report is indicated may ask a court to enter a finding that a child has been abused. If the court makes such a finding, the abuse report is considered founded. A report can also be founded if the perpetrator has pled guilty or been convicted of a criminal charge involving the same factual circumstances involved in the allegation of child abuse. Founded reports are also recorded in the statewide central register.

All reports of suspected child abuse are confidential, but they may be made available to persons who work in the child protective services system or who work with the child, such as the child's physician, the court or law enforcement officials. The child, the child's parent, and the person named in the report as the abuser, are usually also entitled to have access to the abuse report however the report will not contain the name of the reporter of the abuse.

CHILD PROTECTIVE CUSTODY

The agency responsible for investigating child abuse or neglect reports is required to respond to a report within a specified amount of time after the report is received. If it is determined that a child has been abused, neglected, or is in an unsafe environment, the child may be taken into protective custody.

In general, a child may be taken into protective custody without parental consent at a hospital or medical facility, by a physician or medical institution, when it is immediately necessary to protect the child from further serious injury, abuse, or neglect. A child may also be taken into protective custody by law enforcement officials or appointed officers of the court if there are reasonable grounds to believe that the child is suffering from illness or injury or is in imminent danger from his surroundings, and that the child's removal is necessary.

Depending on the jurisdiction, a child protection agency worker may need judicial authorization to take a child into protective custody. The reader is advised to check the law of his or her jurisdiction to determine who is authorized to take a child into protective custody and the circumstances under which a child may be removed.

If the child has been taken into custody by a medical institution or law enforcement agency, the child protective agency must be notified. In addition, the child's parent or guardian must be notified if they are not already aware that the child has been removed.

In general, the child protective agency must secure a court order permitting the child to be kept in custody for any length of time. There must be a hearing to determine whether the child may be returned to his or her parent or whether protective custody should continue. The child protective agency will usually conduct an investigation into the allegations of the report, the child's background and home environment. If the results of the investigation are substantiated, the agency must make appropriate arrangements to safeguard the child, such as placement in a foster care program until the parents are able to properly care for the child, or the provision of necessary services, such as referrals to the appropriate agency when a drug or alcohol problem exists. If the outcome of the investigation is that the report was unsubstantiated, the child may be returned to the home.

STATEWIDE REGISTER

All states maintain some type of registry that identifies perpetrators of child abuse who have been the subject of founded and indicated abuse reports. The register serves as a screening device to prevent perpetrators from being accepted into employment or caregiving situations where they will have extensive contact with children. In general, a person named as a perpetrator in an indicated report has a certain amount of time from the date of notification of the status of the report to request that the state amend or seal the report or remove the report from the statewide register on the grounds that it is inaccurate or that it is being maintained in a manner inconsistent with the law. The finding of an indicated abuse report can be challenged through an administrative hearing and then a court hearing if necessary.

RECENT STATISTICS

According to the United States Department of Health and Human Services, each year, almost 3 million children are alleged to have been abused or neglected, and nearly 1 million are found to have been victims of maltreatment. As of September 30, 1998, an estimated 560,000 children were living in foster care in the United States. The median length of stay for these children was almost 2 years, and more than one-third of these children had been in foster care for 3 or more years. Approximately 122,000 children were unable to return to their parents' homes and were waiting for new permanent families.

The U.S. Department of Health and Human Services report on child maltreatment data is set forth in Appendix 16.

CHAPTER 5:
THE ROLE OF SOCIETY

THE FAMILY

The American family has undergone a variety of changes in the past two decades. The traditional family consisted of two parents—the father and mother—and their biological children, known as the "nuclear family." Today, a "family" may consist of numerous variations of the traditional form.

Divorce and the Broken Family

The major reason for the changing family structure has been the acceptance of, and increase in, divorce in America. Divorce has spawned the era of broken families, such as the "single-parent" family, the "reconstituted" family, and a variety of custodial arrangements affecting the children of a divorced couple. When parents divorce, there is often bitterness and, all too often, an attempt to involve the child. This places added stress on the child, who has no doubt already witnessed more than his or her share of parental disputes.

The Single-Parent Family

A single-parent family is one in which one parent remains the primary caretaker of the children, usually the female, and the children maintain little or no contact with the other parent. Whether the absence of one parental figure—usually the father figure—contributes to delinquency, is still being debated. However, one cannot understate the importance, for example, of a strong male role model for a young impressionable boy. This is recognized in society by the formation of various organizations which attempt to provide this element, such as the Boy Scouts, the Big Brother program, and Little League, to name a few.

The Reconstituted Family

A reconstituted family is one in which the original parent has divorced and remarried. The children of the original marriage may now be members of two distinct families. One or both families may consist of a biological parent, a stepparent and step siblings. This is also known as a blended family.

There has been very little research on the connection between a reconstituted family and delinquency. However, as in any divorce situation, the children carry with them the pain and anger over the breakup of the original family. Having to adjust to a stepparent and new siblings brings added pressure on a child who has already seen his or her family life change dramatically.

In many instances, the stepparent may desire to adopt his or her mate's child. This is most likely when the child is young, and when the whereabouts of the other biological parent are unknown or he or she consents to the stepparent adoption. Depending on the age of the child, his or her consent may be required.

A table setting forth the age at which the child's consent is required for adoption in each state is set forth in Appendix 17.

Quality of Home Life Factor

Statistics show a strong correlation between delinquency and broken families, although it has been shown that the presence of conflict and tension within the family unit, whether intact or broken, is more closely related to delinquency. In particular, it is the quality of the relationship between the parental figures that most affects the children, either positively or negatively.

Thus, for example, a dysfunctional, but intact, traditional family unit is more apt to foster delinquent behavior than a happy, single-parent home. It should also be noted that the presence of delinquent behavior in a home contributes to family conflict and tension, thereby creating a vicious cycle which is difficult to break.

In addition, the degree and quality of parental affection and involvement is strongly related to delinquency. Studies have shown that children who do not receive adequate affection and attention from their parents are more likely to engage in delinquent behavior. This may also account for the fact that delinquency is more prevalent in large families, for whom it may be difficult to give the proper amount of nurturing to each individual child.

The family is where a child is ideally supposed to receive his or her training. The parents are entrusted with the responsibility of teaching the child right from wrong and disciplining improper behavior. When parents are either too busy or disinterested in the daily supervision of their children, the children are more likely to engage in delinquent behavior. However, a child who perceives that the parent is interested in his or her day-to-day activities is more likely to be concerned about displeasing the parent.

THE EDUCATIONAL SYSTEM

Outside of the family, a child's most significant contact is with the educational system. Ideally, schooling is intended to assist the family in its goal of instilling discipline, character, and responsibility in children, as well as transmitting knowledge and skills. In addition, schooling preoccupies a large part of a child's time with positive activities, limiting the child's idle time and resultant opportunity for misbehavior.

Children who are actively and enthusiastically involved in their school work and the extracurricular activities offered simply do not have the time to get into trouble. In fact, studies have shown a correlation between the dislike of school and delinquent behavior.

Truancy

In general, all children who fall between a state's age range for compulsory education is required to attend school on a regular basis. Children generally begin their formal education at age 6. In most states, the maximum age a child is required to attend school is 16.

A table setting forth each state's maximum compulsory education age requirements is set forth in Appendix 18.

Every parent or legal guardian who is responsible for a child between the required ages is liable for making sure that the child attends school regularly. When a child of compulsory school age does not attend school for a certain number of consecutive days—e.g. 3 days—without a valid excuse for the absences the child is considered a truant. A child is considered habitually truant when he or she is absent from school for more than a certain number of school days following his or her first truancy.

In general, before any proceedings are brought against a parent or guardian because of a child's truancy, the parent is entitled to receive written notice of the violation. The notice generally comes from the school district superintendent or other person in charge of the school district's attendance policy. The school district then files a truancy petition in Family Court and a truancy hearing is scheduled.

Depending on the jurisdiction, if the Court finds that a child is a truant, the child's parent or guardian can be found guilty and fined and/or may be required to complete a parenting education program. In some states, if the parent or guardian fails to comply with the court order, they can be sentenced to serve time in jail.

Punishing a parent for a child's truancy, particularly where they are dealing with an older child, may be unfair if the parent has taken all reasonable steps to make sure the child attends school. In such cases, the court will generally consider the individual circumstances of each case in determining whether the actions of a parent or guardian were reasonable and whether they should be held responsible for the child's actions.

A truant child may be arrested by a law enforcement officer or other person authorized to arrest truant children. When the child is arrested, the person taking the child into custody must promptly notify the parents. The child may be taken to the school in which the child is enrolled. If the child is found to be habitually truant, the child may be referred by the school district to the Family Court at which time the child may be adjudicated a status offender for violating the state's compulsory education law.

If it is deemed that the child is in need of services, the Court may order the child removed from his or her home and placed in a juvenile facility or group home during which time the child must attend school. Early intervention into truant behavior is crucial as studies have shown a correlation between dropping out of school and delinquent behavior.

Disciplinary Action and Due Process

Disruptive—and often criminal—behavior has become a serious problem in modern day schools, particularly in large urban cities. Although much of the criminal behavior is nonviolent, such as vandalism and theft, there has also been an alarming increase in violent offenses against teachers, as well as other students, often involving weapons. Many schools have had to hire additional security personnel, and install safety devices, such as weapon detectors, in an effort to protect the students and teachers. School violence is discussed in more detail in Chapter 3 of this almanac.

The right to receive an education has been recognized as a property right. Therefore, according to the United States Supreme Court, when a public school student is accused of offensive behavior, whether as minor as smoking on school grounds or as serious as selling drugs on school grounds, the child is entitled to a certain level of protection—known as "due process"—before he or she may be deprived of the right to an education.

According to the Fourteenth Amendment to the Constitution, all persons—including students—are entitled to due process of law. Due process generally means that a government official—including a public school official—cannot unilaterally take disciplinary action against a student without first providing a hearing. This right was established in 1975, in *Goss v. Lopez*, when the U.S. Supreme Court held that some high school students were improperly suspended without benefit of a hearing. Further, public school officials cannot take disproportionately severe action against a student for a relatively minor violation.

Nevertheless, students do not have the right to a hearing if the punishment is minor, such as detention. Further, if it is determined that the student is a danger to school property or to other students, suspension or expulsion may proceed. However, notice of the charges and a hearing must be held as soon thereafter as possible.

Short-Term Suspension

Where the infraction leads to suspension from school which is considered short-term—up to 10 consecutive days—the required due process is minimal, and includes the requirement that notice of the infraction, either written or spoken, be given to the offender, and that the offender be given the chance to have his or her defense heard. Before a student is disciplined, many states require that there be an informal hearing in which the student meets with a school official, such as the principal. Most such cases are resolved at this level between the student and his or her parents and the school officials.

Even when there is clear evidence that a suspension is unjustified, it is impractical to take legal action to stop the suspension because of its short duration. Under the Family Education Rights and Privacy Act (FERPA), however, the student has the right to have his or her transcript corrected. If the disciplinary action was racially motivated, legal action for civil rights violations and damages also may be warranted.

Long-Term Suspension or Expulsion

When the disciplinary action is more severe, such as long-term suspension—over 10 days—or expulsion, a student is entitled to additional protection, including a formal hearing, usually held before the board of education. The student, and the parents of a minor child, are entitled to written notice of: the time and place of the hearing, the nature of the allegations, and the student's rights, including the right to counsel, the right to present evidence, the right to confront witnesses, and the right to a written decision. The school has the burden of proving its case. In addition, the student has the right to appeal an adverse decision to a higher authority, such as the state's courts.

Corporal Punishment

Approximately 21 states have banned corporal punishment in the school setting. Some states still permit corporal punishment, but define the circumstances under which it may be undertaken. In addition, the punishment must not be "unreasonable and unnecessary" or "excessive." Corporal punishment is not permitted if the parents disagree with this form of disciplinary measure.

School Searches

In their 1985 decision in *New Jersey v. T.L.O.*, the U.S. Supreme Court ruled that school officials may search students without a warrant when they have reasonable grounds for suspecting that the search will turn up evidence that the student has violated the law, or rules of the school. However, school officials may not conduct a search unless they have a good reason to believe that the individual being searched is the one who broke the law or the school rule.

Strip Searches

All searches must be conducted in a reasonable manner, taking into consideration the student's age. Strip searches are illegal in many states. If a state permits strip searching a student, they must be prepared to justify the search based on the severity of the suspected offense.

School Lockers

States are split on the issue of whether school lockers can be legally searched without cause. Some states have found a privacy interest in a student's locker and require school officials to have some reasonable basis to suspect that there is something illegal in the locker before they can search it. Case law has held that the search of student property is permissible where the school officials have a reasonable suspicion that an infraction has occurred and the search is related to that suspicion. Since lockers are considered school property, school officials generally have the right to search lockers where there is reasonable suspicion. Some states provide that merely because a student locker is considered school property it is searchable and they are not subject to the reasonable suspicion test.

Dress Codes

The right to enforce a dress code on the student body depends upon the state. The reader is advised to check the law of his or her own jurisdiction.

Drug and Alcohol Testing

The right of school officials to administer drug and alcohol tests to students depends on the state. The reader is advised to check the law of his or her own jurisdiction in this regard.

Student Athletes

In their 1995 decision in *Vernonia v. Acton*, the U.S. Supreme Court held that student athletes are subject to drug and alcohol testing because athletic programs are voluntary and student athletes are role models for the student body.

Censorship

The First Amendment guarantees the individual's right to free expression and free association. In their 1969 decision in *Tinker v. Des Moines Independent Community School District*, the U.S. Supreme Court held that public school students in public schools are also guaranteed their First Amendment rights to free expression and association. Therefore, students have the right to express their opinions, provided they do so in a way that doesn't "materially and substantially" disrupt school activities.

Case law has set certain standards when it comes to the student's exercise of free speech in the school setting. A student whose speech is particularly disruptive due to its content is subject to disciplinary action. This is necessary because school officials are entrusted to maintain a safe and orderly environment in the school setting.

Student Publication

A school is generally not permitted to censor a student publication provided it is not "indecent" and does not "materially and substantially" disrupt school activities.

Official School Publication

School officials do have more control over official school papers. Case law has upheld the right of school officials to revise material contained in school newspapers, particularly when the publication is produced in class as part of the curriculum and when the desire to control student expression is related to legitimate educational concerns. In their 1988 decision in *Hazelwood School District v. Kuhlmeier*, the U.S. Supreme Court held that public school administrators can censor student speech in official school publications or activities if the officials think students are saying something "inappropriate" or "harmful" even if it is not vulgar and does not disrupt school activities.

School Library Censorship

In their 1982 ruling in *Island Trees v. Pico*, the U.S. Supreme Court held that school officials cannot remove books from the school library simply because they disagree with the content. Nevertheless, schools are entitled to select the books they think have the greatest value for their students and to reject those that they believe have little value.

Gender Discrimination

Public schools are prohibited from providing academic courses to only one gender, and are required to provide both boys and girls with equal athletic opportunities. Nevertheless, many courts have held that having separate teams for boys and girls is permissible provided the school gives students of both genders equal chance to participate in the same sport.

Metal Detectors

Many states permit school officials to install metal detectors to prevent students from bringing weapons into the school. The courts have generally held that metal detectors are legal, provided they are not used in a discriminatory manner, e.g., only requiring male or minority students to pass through the metal detectors.

The Pledge of Allegiance

The Supreme Court has held that requiring students to recite The Pledge of Allegiance violates The First Amendment. Thus, a student has the right to remain silently seated during the pledge.

Pregnant Students

The Federal law prohibits schools from discriminating against pregnant students, married students, and students with children. For example, school officials cannot prevent a pregnant student from attending regular school classes, even if the school provides segregated classes for pregnant students. In addition, school officials cannot prevent a pregnant student from engaging in extracurricular activities, unless there is a valid health reason, e.g., the activity would endanger the health of the fetus or expectant mother.

Student Records

Schools maintain records of a student's academic and personal progress from kindergarten through graduation which include, among other things, grades, progress reports, psychological reports, and teacher evaluations. According to the Family Educational Rights and Privacy Act of 1974 (FERPA), schools that receive any federal funding must make student records available for viewing by parents and legal guardians, and by the students themselves provided they are age 18 or older.

In general, schools are entitled to release student records to teachers and school officials who have a legitimate educational interest in the records, e.g., if the student transfers. Permission from the student's parents is generally required prior to the release of the records.

Nevertheless, a school may be allowed to release a student record without obtaining permission in emergency situations where the information is necessary to protect the student's health and safety, or the health and safety of the other students.

Inaccurate or irrelevant information contained in a student's record, such as subjective remarks by teachers, may be changed or deleted from the record upon request. If school officials refuse to change or delete the information, a formal hearing must be held before an impartial third party. If it is determined that there is to be no change to the record, the student and his or her parents can request that a statement be added to the record which expresses disagreement with the information.

CHAPTER 6:
EMANCIPATION

THE AGE OF MAJORITY

It has long been held that children lack competence to make important decisions that affect their lives and, by law, they are prohibited from making many of those important decisions until they reach the state-established age of majority. The majority of states have specified 18 as the age of majority.

A table depicting the age of majority by state is set forth in Appendix 19.

These statutes are intended to protect children. For example, a child cannot enter into a binding contract and cannot bring a lawsuit on his or her own behalf. This protects the child both from making his or her own mistakes, due to lack of experience and judgment, and from those who may try to use the child's inexperience to exploit the child.

Generally, the statutes do not distinguish between the younger child and the older child, nor do they make special provisions for the child who exhibits the maturity and capacity to make his or her own decisions. However, there has been a trend towards selective emancipation—i.e., shifting some of the decisions which were previously exclusively under parental control to the child, as more fully explained below.

SELECTIVE EMANCIPATION

It has been deemed that a child, upon reaching a statutorily designated age below the state's age of majority, should have the right to make his or her own decisions in certain limited situations without the consent of his or her parents or the state. Most of the selective emancipation statutes deal with personal matters, such as a child's right to seek birth control, pregnancy testing, and treatment for venereal disease. Such exceptions are rooted in the United States Supreme Court's determination that certain decisions involve a fundamental and constitutionally protected right to privacy, which has been deemed to apply to minors as well as adults.

COMPLETE EMANCIPATION

In General

Emancipation is the legal process by which a minor can attain legal adulthood before reaching the statutory age of majority. Emancipation basically refers to the release of a minor from parental control. A child who feels he or she is unable to live under the control of his or her parents may petition the court for emancipation, under the state's child emancipation statute or its common law.

Emancipation Petition

A petition for emancipation by a minor must generally state that:

1. The minor has moved out of his or her parents' home.

2. The minor is not receiving financial support from his or her parents.

3. The minor is capable of responsibly controlling his or her own actions and does so.

The minor should be as specific as possible about how long he or she has been living independently and how self-support is achieved. When the court considers the emancipation petition, the minor's parents will be notified and will be invited to attend the hearing and speak at the hearing on their view about the child's request for emancipation.

The decision as to whether to grant the minor's petition for emancipation is generally held to be a question of fact. This means that a judge will look at all of the minor's circumstances to determine whether the minor is able to live on his or her own as an adult. A judge will usually consider the following factors: age, marital status, ability to be self-supportive, and the minor's desire to live independently of his or her parents. The court will consider whether the minor is employed and has a stable source of income as well as a place to live. If the court finds that emancipation is in the child's best interests, and that the child is sufficiently mature to carry on his or her own affairs, the court may grant the minor's petition for emancipation. The judge will issue a court decree of emancipation, and the minor can get a copy for his or her records to prove his or her status.

However, emancipation is not available in every state, and in those states that provide for emancipation, the laws differ among the states.

A list of state emancipation statutes is set forth in Appendix 20.

Role of Parents

Emancipation is a very serious step since it frees the minor's parents of responsibilities to the child, and from any further obligation to support the child. Nevertheless, depending on the jurisdiction, a minor remains emancipated only as long as he or she remains financially independent of his or her parents, free of their care and control, and living independently. If the act which conferred emancipation ends while the child is still a minor, the child may once again become a dependent of his or her parents until he or she reaches the age of majority and is generally no longer considered emancipated.

For example, in many states, a minor who enlists in the military with parental consent at 17 is only emancipated for the period of time he or she is in the service. If the child is discharged prior to the state's age of majority, the child is again considered a dependent minor.

MARRIAGE

There are certain actions a child may take prior to reaching the age of majority that remove the impediments of minority and legally allow the child to make his or her own decisions as an adult. For example, if a child marries, depending on the jurisdiction, he or she may be considered "emancipated" and no longer under the control of his or her parents. By the same token, the parents may no longer obligated for the support of the child.

However, the marriage itself does not emancipate a minor for all purposes in all jurisdictions and the marriage is but one factor among the minor's whole situation that a judge will consider when determining whether the minor should be emancipated. The fact that a minor is married usually demonstrates that he or she is independent of his or her parents, but there are some cases where this is not so. Therefore the court must consider other factors in addition to marital status to determine whether the minor is living independently and is self-supportive. When minor married couples live away from their parents and support themselves, they satisfy the general standard of emancipation. If minors divorce or obtain an annulment, however, they can also revert to unemancipated status.

Nevertheless, if a minor child wishes to marry, he or she cannot do so without the consent of a parent. If parental consent is withheld, the child may petition the court to overrule the parent's decision and grant emancipation. The age at which parental consent is no longer needed to marry is often the same as the state's specified age of majority.

A table showing the ages at which a child may marry with and without parental consent in each state is set forth in Appendix 21.

MINOR PARENTS

A minor parent acquires rights similar to adults with respect to his or her own child as long as the minor parent cares for the child adequately. However, becoming a parent does not emancipate a minor for all purposes. If a minor is not self-supportive, and does not live independently of his or her parents, the minor is not considered emancipated, whether or not they are a parent.

Nevertheless, as further discussed in Chapter 7, minors do acquire some of the rights of adults when they have a child. For example, minor parents have the right to custody of their child and to make decisions regarding the child's upbringing, such as consenting to medical treatment, educational planning, and adoption. Minor parents maintain these rights regardless of whether they live with their own parents or not, as long as they adequately care for their child.

Limitations

Emancipation does not mean being treated like an adult in all situations. For example, emancipated minors cannot vote or drink alcoholic beverages. Further, emancipated minors' signatures on contracts are not binding in the same way as those of adults.

Independent Unemancipated Minors

It is legal for an unemancipated minor to live independently or with an adult friend or relative, with the consent of the minor's parent or guardian, provided the minor's health or safety is not endangered. This, however, does not mean that the minor is emancipated. In these situations, the parent or legal guardian is still ultimately legally responsible for the minor's welfare and his or her actions.

If a minor moves out of the home of his or her parent or legal guardian without their consent, the minor is considered a runaway and can be picked up by authorities. Depending on the circumstances, the minor may be referred to the Family Court and can be placed in a juvenile facility or group home if the parents are unable to control the minor.

CHAPTER 7:
TEENAGE PREGNANCY

IN GENERAL

America has the highest rate of teenage pregnancy, childbirth and abortion in the industrialized world. Ironically, the teenagers who are having babies are the least able, financially and emotionally, to raise a child. Statistically, the profile of the typical teenage mother is one who is poor, unemployed, uneducated, and living in a single-parent family. The increased responsibility of caring for a child often deters the teenage mother from seeking employment or an education, therefore, the family is usually trapped by poverty on a long-term basis. In fact, as shown below, recent studies have found a correlation between poverty and teenage pregnancy and birth rates.

STATISTICS

Nearly 1 million American teenagers—about 10 percent of all 15- to 19-year-old females—become pregnant each year. About a third abort their pregnancies, 14 percent miscarry, and 52 percent bear children, 72 percent of them out of wedlock.

Of the half million teens who give birth, approximately 75 percent are first-time mothers. More than 175,000 are 17 years old or younger. Studies have shown that these young mothers and their children are especially vulnerable to severe adverse social and economic consequences. More than 80 percent of these young mothers end up in poverty and on welfare, many for the majority of their children's critically important developmental years.

ABORTION

Approximately 32 states require parental notification prior to terminating the pregnancy of an adolescent. The majority of those state statutes also have a provision that requires parental consent for an abortion. The father's consent is not required nor does he have a right to be notified.

Previously, when challenged, state statutes requiring parental consent for termination of pregnancy by adolescents were routinely struck down by the United States Supreme Court as being an unconstitutional violation of the right of privacy. However, in the spring of 1990, the Supreme Court ruled that the Minnesota and Ohio statutes which require parental consent were constitutional. The laws were upheld because they contain a judicial bypass clause, allowing the teenager to seek judicial permission for an abortion, as an alternative to informing the parents. The Supreme Court ruled that the judicial bypass provision was a sufficient guarantee of privacy and freedom.

The right to decide whether to have an abortion belongs to the pregnant woman. Thus, except in a medical emergency where the teenager's life is at risk, no parent or guardian may force a minor to have an abortion. If a teenage girl feels threatened that this may happen, she can go to the court for assistance. An attorney will be appointed for the pregnant girl and the court will grant whatever relief is appropriate to protect the health and welfare of the teenager and her unborn baby.

In those jurisdictions which require parental consent for an abortion, if a parent refuses to consent or if the minor does not want to ask for his or her consent, the minor may petition the Court for permission. In such a case, only a court can authorize a physician to perform the abortion. A judicial decree authorizing the physician to perform an abortion without parental consent can be issued if the court determines that the minor has given informed consent and is a mature minor, is emancipated, or that it would be in the minor's best interest.

In general, if assistance in drafting the petition is needed by the minor, it will be provided by the court. A minor can choose to represent herself at the hearing on her petition, but an attorney will be provided by the court if the minor needs representation. Due to the nature of the petition, the Court is required to make a ruling within a very short period of time— e.g., 3 days—and the time for an appeal of an unfavorable decision is similarly shortened.

ADOPTION

Teenage parents can generally consent to the adoption of their child without their own parents' consent. If the father is not married to the mother—known as a "putative father" —he can generally sign a consent to have the baby adopted at any time. However, the mother typically must wait until after the baby is born to sign the consent and relinquish her parental rights. To be valid, the consent must be "voluntary, intelligent, and deliberate," which means that the consent must not be forced or accepted without presenting the mother with sufficient information about what termination of parental rights will mean and what alternatives and services exist for teen parents. Thus, the minor's parents cannot force the minor to place the baby for adoption. The law may require that the minor's parents be notified of the hearing at which the minor's parental rights will be terminated.

THE RIGHTS OF TEENAGE PARENTS

Teenagers who have children generally have the same rights as adult parents. Teen parents have the right to custody of their child. Further, a minor who has been married or has had a child can give effective consent to medical, dental, and health services for his or her child. However, as discussed in Chapter 6, teenagers who are under the age of majority must have the consent of a parent or a judge if they want to marry.

If a parent is not living up to his or her obligations to support the child, the other parent can sue for support. The court will establish a sum of money that the parent will be required to pay to support his or her child according to the Uniform Child Support Guidelines, which is calculated as a percentage of the parents' gross salary and certain "add-ons" such as child care expenses. The Court will also consider and make decisions about how the parents will provide health care coverage for the child.

ACCESS TO PRENATAL CARE AND MEDICAL SERVICES

A teenager who is pregnant is generally able to consent to her own medical care, including prenatal care. The medical care is generally paid for through private health insurance or the public assistance program operated by the state. If a teenager has private health insurance, she should investigate what kinds of services and coverage the insurance provides in pregnancy. Many states also run other federally funded programs to assist teenage mothers with prenatal health care, parenting classes, and treatment for newborns and young children. A teenager's parents remain financially responsible for her whether or not she is pregnant unless she is legally emancipated.

THE FATHER'S PATERNAL RIGHTS

In general, a father's parental rights are based on marriage to the mother or the establishment of paternity. Placing the father's name on the birth certificate does not in and of itself establish paternity. Biological fathers who have demonstrated a commitment to the responsibilities of parenthood do have an interest in their child, however, this does not guarantee parental rights. If a man's parental rights are established, he has the same rights to the child as the mother.

If the mother and father are married when the child is born, the father's parental rights are clearly established. If the mother then seeks to relinquish her rights to the child, the father does not lose his parental rights and can contest any attempt the mother makes to have the child adopted. As long as the father is able to care for the child, he will maintain his parental rights.

If the mother and father are not married, the father can acknowledge paternity by filing a petition with the Family Court in order to preserve his rights. Once the father acknowledges paternity, he will have the same rights and responsibilities towards the child as the mother, such as providing support. In addition, the mother will not have to do anything further to establish paternity.

If the father has not filed a paternity petition and the mother has begun adoption proceedings, the father must either appear in court when he receives notice of the hearing or file a written objection to the termination of his rights before the hearing takes place.

TEENAGE PARENTS AND PUBLIC ASSISTANCE

The welfare reform laws have affected the eligibility of teenage parents for relief. The Personal Responsibility and Work Opportunity Reconciliation Act of 1996 (PRWORA) is the federal law which governs how welfare benefits are distributed. Title I of PRWORA created the Temporary Assistance to Needy Families (TANF) program, which replaced Aid to Families with Dependent Children (AFDC). The new law requires that each state put a five-year lifetime limit on an individual's (or family's) receipt of TANF. The law also requires that recipients of TANF must find work within two years of receiving assistance, although there are some exceptions for those attending school or training programs. However, the federal law prohibits states from penalizing any parent with children under the age of six who cannot meet work requirements due to lack of available child care.

To receive TANF benefits, a teenage parent must either live at home with his or her parents, a legal guardian, or other adult relative who is at least 18 years old, or in an adult-supervised supportive living arrangement. In addition, the minor parent must attend an educational program directed towards attaining a high school diploma or its equivalent, such as a GED program, to receive public assistance benefits.

In such situations, it is the parent, legal guardian, relative or other adult who is the payee on behalf of the minor parent and his or her child. If the minor parent is unable to return to the home of a parent, legal guardian or other adult relative, the appropriate agency will provide assistance to the minor parent to find an adult-supervised supportive living arrangement.

In general, a minor parent can claim an exemption from the requirement to live with an adult if she can provide documentation as follows:

1. Neither a parent, legal guardian or other adult relative is able to retain or assume parental control over the minor parent due to physical, emotional, mental, financial or other limitations;

2. The minor has no living parent or guardian or their whereabouts are unknown;

3. The parent or guardian of the minor will not let her live in the home due to space, housing code or lease limitations;

4. The physical or emotional health or safety of the minor or her child would be jeopardized if they resided with the parent or guardian, as shown by records from health facilities, school, social service agencies, the police or the courts;

5. The minor parent's child was conceived as result of rape or incest committed by someone living in the household;

6. The minor parent and child no longer reside in the home of the parent or legal guardian because of physical or sexual abuse of the minor parent, her child or any other child in the household or the threat of such abuse;

7. The parent or guardian lives in another area of the state in which it is not practical for the minor parent to live because of factors such as attendance at school, a vocational program, employment, therapy or substance abuse treatment; or

8. The parent, legal guardian or adult relative has spent the minor parent's assistance in an improper manner.

Additional exemptions will be granted if they are deemed in the best interests of the minor and her child at the discretion of the appropriate social services agency. If the minor parent meets one of the above exceptions, the minor parent becomes the payee for public assistance benefits unless an appropriate adult supervised placement is found.

To receive financial assistance, the teenage mother must cooperate with the appropriate social services agency in identifying the father for support purposes unless the teenage mother can claim "good cause" not to identify the father. Circumstances under which "good cause" may arise include a reasonable expectation that pursuit of a paternity action would result in serious physical or emotional harm to either the child, the minor mother, or the caretaker of the minor mother and child; the child was conceived through incest or rape; or adoption proceedings are pending.

A good cause claim must be supported by documentation, including medical, law enforcement, social services, and psychological records. A sworn statement of an individual other than the applicant or recipient with knowledge of the circumstances can also be used to support a good cause claim. The agency may then conduct an investigation of the claim.

CORRELATION BETWEEN TEENAGE PREGNANCY AND JUVENILE DELINQUENCY

The Office of Juvenile Justice and Delinquency Prevention (OJJDP) is responsible for leading the national fight against juvenile violence and victimization. Among other activities, OJJDP supports research on the causes of delinquency and disseminates information on a variety of juvenile justice issues.

According to recent studies, male children of teenage mothers are 2.7 times more likely to be incarcerated than the sons of mothers who delay childbearing until their early 20's. Young men born to teenage mothers are incarcerated at the rate of 10.3 percent compared to a 3.8 rate for young men born to mothers who began their families at age 20 or 21. The national average regardless of the age of the parent is 5 percent.

In addition, studies have demonstrated a correlation between child abuse and neglect and teenage childbearing. Some studies have shown that children born to adolescent mothers were twice as likely to become victims of abuse and neglect than children born to older mothers.

CHAPTER 8:
ADDITIONAL AGE-RELATED ISSUES
AND RESTRICTIONS

IN GENERAL

In addition to the statutory disabilities of a child who has not yet reached the age of majority, as discussed in Chapter 4, the government has placed additional age-related limitations on the activities minors may be permitted to engage in, such as working, driving, drinking alcohol, and smoking. The reason for these limitations is much the same as the reason for establishing the age of majority—to protect the child from harm by limiting his or her ability to participate in those activities the child is not yet prepared to participate in due to inexperience or immature judgment. Some of these age-related restrictions are discussed below.

EMPLOYMENT

Prior to industrialization, the training of children in various occupations, usually by apprenticeship, was considered a very important factor in a child's development. The child learned responsibility and a trade which was to sustain him or her in adulthood. After industrialization took hold in America, the type of work that children were engaged in changed dramatically. Children were sent to work in factories, on assembly lines, and in very unhealthy and dangerous environments. The working conditions were unregulated and children were seen as a valuable source of inexpensive labor.

In the late nineteenth century, various states attempted to enact and reform their child labor laws. However, these laws were not uniform and the exploitation of child labor was still prevalent in many states. This resulted in unfair competition among the states, since the states with stricter child labor laws were at a disadvantage in the economic marketplace. Manufacturers were more likely to set up their operations in those states that did not regulate child labor.

It became apparent that federal legislation would be necessary to resolve the child labor problem and, in 1938, Congress enacted the Fair Labor Standards Act (FLSA). In general, the FLSA prohibits the use of "oppressive child labor in commerce, or in any enterprise engaged in commerce, or in the production of goods for commerce." The FLSA set forth the minimum ages at which minors could be employed in various occupations, depending on the level of danger or hazard surrounding the particular job. Nevertheless, the FLSA contained so many exemptions that its effectiveness was severely limited. Currently, every state has some form of child labor law regulating the employment of minors.

A table setting forth the minimum child employment age in each state is set forth in Appendix 22.

TEENAGE SMOKING

Smoking has been under attack for some time now, and the health-related risks associated with smoking, such as throat and lung cancer, have been widely publicized. This activity has been banned in restaurants and other public places, and in most workplaces, due to the public's concern over the effects of secondhand smoke on people who have decided not to subject themselves to the health risks of smoking. Most experts and healthcare professionals agree that nicotine is unquestionably the most addictive drug in use today.

Nevertheless, over 1 million children start smoking every year. Of that number, approximately one-half will become addicted. Unfortunately, children do not consider the long-term health effects of smoking, despite media campaigns, warning labels, and school intervention programs.

A child is more likely to smoke if his or her parents smoke. In addition, peer pressure, teenage rebellion, curiosity and a desire to feel sophisticated and "grown up" contribute to the decision to start smoking. In large part, the tobacco companies have also added to the problem of teenage smoking. There has been much controversy over cigarette advertising that seems to be marketed towards children, such as the use of cartoon character spokespersons. In addition, tobacco companies often sponsor events which draw young people, such as rock concerts, and distribute promotional items, such as T-shirts, designed to appeal to teenagers.

Tobacco companies have been accused of attempting to replace the loss of adult consumers by trying to influence children at their most vulnerable age, thereby ensuring a future generation of smokers. Although companies vigorously deny this charge, it is a fact that half of all adult smokers start by age 13, and 25% start by age 11. Studies have shown that the younger one starts to smoke, the more difficult it is to quit.

Thus, laws have had to be established to make it illegal to provide a minor with cigarettes, and criminal penalties may be assessed against anyone for selling or furnishing cigarettes to a minor. It is illegal in most states for a minor to purchase cigarettes.

A table containing the minimum age at which minors may purchase cigarettes in each state is set forth in Appendix 23.

DRIVING

In General

When a child reaches a certain age, it becomes difficult for them to rely on their parents to transport them to their many and various activities. For example, older children frequently work and may need to drive to get back and forth from their place of employment, particularly if they live in a suburban or rural area. Therefore, the states have generally established an age which is lower than the state's statutory age of majority at which a child can qualify for a driver's license under certain circumstances, as well as other restrictions applicable to the young driver.

Because driving requires demonstration of a certain level of responsibility, both to protect the young driver and those with whom he or she may come in contact, the states have generally imposed certain requirements on the minor license applicant which are not required of adults. For example, a child may be required to take a driver education training course before qualifying for a junior license. In addition, the state may suspend or revoke a minor's license under circumstances and for violations that would not be applicable to an adult.

A table setting forth state laws applicable to young drivers is set forth in Appendix 24.

Statistics

As a group, teenage drivers are disproportionately involved in motor vehicle crashes worldwide. In 1996, 5,805 teenagers died in the United States from motor vehicle crash injuries. Such injuries are by far the leading public health problem for young people 13-19 years old. Thirty-four percent of all deaths of 16-19 year-olds from all causes are related to motor vehicles.

In addition to teenage drivers, many teenagers die as passengers in motor vehicles. Sixty-three percent of teenage passenger deaths in 1996 occurred in crashes in which another teenager was driving. Teenagers far exceed all other age groups in terms of per capita deaths as both drivers and passengers, but their passenger fatality rates are much more extreme compared with those of older drivers.

Immaturity and lack of driving experience are the main reasons. Compared with older drivers, teenagers as a group are more willing to take risks and less likely to use safety belts. They are also more likely than older drivers to underestimate the dangers associated with hazardous situations and less able to cope with such dangers. Analyses of fatal crash data indicate that teenage drivers are more likely to be at fault in their crashes.

Beginner Drivers

Most beginner drivers are 16 years old when they qualify for a driver's license, a relatively easy undertaking for such a great responsibility. Applicants for a first driver's license in all states must meet vision, knowledge, and skills requirements. Only thirty-five states and the District of Columbia require beginner drivers to obtain learner's permits before getting their driver's licenses. Only 23 of those states require the permit to be held for a minimum period, ranging from 10 days to 1 year. In most states, new permit holders may immediately apply for licenses. Once licensed, young, inexperienced and often immature drivers in most states are permitted to drive unrestricted.

Ironically, statistics have demonstrated that this age group is at the highest risk of having a serious automobile accident. In addition, the youngest drivers have the worst record in terms of passenger deaths. More teenage passenger deaths occur when a 16 year-old is driving than any other age group.

The combination of inexperience behind the wheel and immaturity has contributed to the highest percentage of crashes involving speeding and driver error for this age group, as well as the highest fatal crash rate for single vehicles and high-occupancy vehicles. In 1996, a total of 1,539 people died in crashes involving 16-year-old drivers, including 572 16-year old drivers, 498 passengers, 366 occupants of other vehicles, and 89 pedestrians.

A number of factors have been found to contribute to the high incidence of accidents involving 16-year olds, including (i) driver error; (ii) speeding (iii) failure to use seat belts; (iv) high occupancy vehicles; and (v) alcohol use.

Driver Error

The most significant factor in accidents involving 16-year olds is driver error. Eighty-two percent of 16-year-old drivers in fatal crashes during 1996 made at least one driving error that contributed to the crashes. This compares with 68 percent of drivers 17-19 years old and 52 percent of drivers 25-49 years old.

In addition, forty-one percent of the fatal crashes involving 16-year-old drivers were single vehicle accidents. The vehicle generally left the road and overturned or struck an object like a tree or pole. Among 16-year-old drivers, this is by far the most frequent type of accident. In contrast, only 27 percent of fatal crashes with 25-49 year-olds at the wheel in 1996 were single-vehicle.

Speeding

Another common problem among this age group is speeding. Police reports indicate that 36 percent of all 16-year-old drivers in fatal crashes during 1996 were reportedly speeding or, if not exceeding the limit, going too fast for road conditions. This proportion drops steadily with age—only 21 percent of drivers 25-49 years old were reportedly speeding when their fatal crashes occurred in 1996.

Failure to Use Seat Belts

Statistics have indicated that many of the 16 year-olds in fatal crashes did not use seat belts.

High Occupancy Vehicles

Sixty-three percent of teenage passenger deaths in 1996 occurred in crashes in which another teenager was driving. Fatal crashes involving drivers this age are much more likely to occur with three or more occupants in the vehicle than are crashes involving older drivers. The occupants are usually other teenagers. In 1996, 36 percent of all crashes involving 16-year-old drivers happened when there were three or more people in the vehicle.

Alcohol Use

Statistics indicate that alcohol is not a big factor in accidents involving beginner drivers, unlike older teens and adults. Only 15 percent of all 16-year-old drivers killed in 1996 crashes had blood alcohol concentrations above 0.10 percent. This compares with 32 percent for older teenagers, and 53 percent for drivers 25-49 years old. However, although young drivers are less likely to drink and drive, their crash rate is substantially higher when they do.

The problem of underage drinking and driving is discussed more fully in Chapter 3 of this almanac.

Graduated Licensing Laws

As set forth above, under most state laws, beginning teenage drivers may get very little experience before they can obtain a license that permits unrestricted driving. Training and education programs, such as high school driver education, can help teens learn driving skills, but unfortunately it has been demonstrated that they don't produce safer drivers. More often than not it is the attitude, and not the skills, of the teen driver that are the problem. Teenagers tend to think of themselves as invincible. They generally believe they "know it all" and resist adult standards and regulations.

The success of graduated licensing systems for teenage drivers abroad has led to the introduction of similar programs in a number of states. Florida and Michigan have enacted graduated licensing programs, and plans to introduce similar programs are underway in California, Georgia, Illinois, Louisiana, New Hampshire, and North Carolina. Surveys have demonstrated that the majority of parents are generally in favor of such programs.

Studies have indicated that the most productive policies in effect to reduce teen accidents are those that restrict teenagers' driving exposure. For example, curfews that apply to all late-night activities for 13-17 year-olds have been show to reduce crashes and crash injuries.

Graduated licensing is intended to control the progression from beginner driver to unrestricted driving, lifting restrictions one by one until a young driver "graduates" to full licensure. Restrictions typically include limits on teen passengers, and a prohibition on night driving. Graduated licensing systems may also include special sanctions to discourage moving violations, belt law violations, and alcohol violations.

During the learner's phase, driving isn't permitted unless there's an adult supervisor. In the intermediate phase, young licensees are allowed to drive unsupervised under some conditions but not others. For example, supervision is required when driving in the late night and early morning hours.

Night driving curfews are an important element of graduated licensing systems. Most night driving curfews in force in the United States allow exemptions for driving to work or school during the restricted hours. Graduated licensing introduces unrestricted night driving only after on-the-road experience is gained during the day.

Graduated licensing is designed to introduce beginners into the driving population in a low-risk manner, protecting both them and others they meet on the roads. Graduated licensing systems could apply to all first-time drivers, not just the youngest, as they do outside the United States. In the United States, however, young people make up the majority of beginning drivers, and graduated licensing systems now being considered in some states would focus on these drivers.

Studies indicate that parents are strongly in favor of graduated licensing. A 1994 Insurance Institute for Highway Safety survey of 1,000 parents of 17 year-olds found that 90 percent favored a minimum period of supervised driving before full licensure, 74 percent favored night driving curfews, 43 percent favored restricting teenage passengers during the first few months of driving, and 97 percent favored a zero BAC for teenagers.

Fifty-eight percent of parents said they favored a graduated licensing package including many months of supervised driving practice before licensing, a night driving curfew, and prohibitions against transporting other teenagers until a good driving record has been demonstrated for six months to a year.

Graduated licensing systems have demonstrated that they are effective in reducing the motor vehicle injury risk for young people. In the states that have elements of graduated licensing, the safety benefits are evident. Studies of night driving curfews indicate that crash reductions of 60 percent or more can be achieved during curfew hours.

The National Committee on Uniform Traffic Laws and Ordinances (NCUTLO)

The National Transportation Safety Board, National Highway Traffic Safety Administration, and Insurance Institute for Highway Safety classify the licensing systems of the 50 states and District of Columbia according to the specifications of a widely accepted model graduated licensing law developed by the National Committee on Uniform Traffic Laws and Ordinances (NCUTLO).

NCUTLO's model law specifies core provisions for graduated licensing. The core provisions of the NCUTLO model include (i) a learner's phase of at least six months, followed by (ii) an intermediate phase of at least six months, and (iii) a prohibition of unsupervised driving at night for young drivers during the intermediate phase.

The NCUTLO model requires applicants for intermediate and full licenses to have no "seat belt" or "zero tolerance" alcohol use violations, and to otherwise be conviction free during the mandatory holding periods. The model recognizes that states may define "conviction free" to include only serious violations and may suspend offenders or provide lesser penalties. In most states with graduated licensing, violations by young drivers result in license suspension or extension of the holding periods.

The NCUTLO model recommends a minimum age of 16 for a learner's permit, and prohibits unsupervised driving from 10 p.m. to 5 a.m. However, failure to include these provisions does not disqualify a state from satisfying NCUTLO's core provisions.

There are a number of provisions not included in the NCUTLO model which have been proposed by other agencies. For example, the model does not include two-stage driver education to coincide with the phases of graduated licensing, as recommended by the National Highway Traffic

Safety Administration. In addition, the NCUTLO model does not impose passenger restrictions during the intermediate phase, nor does it require parents or others to certify completion of a minimum number of hours of supervised driving in the learner's phase. However, the NCUTLO model does recommend certification of supervised driving in states that do not mandate any driver education.

APPENDIX 1:
STATE MINIMUM AND MAXIMUM AGE REQUIREMENTS FOR ORIGINAL JURISDICTION IN DELINQUENCY MATTERS

STATE	MINIMUM AGE	MAXIMUM AGE
Alabama	unspecified	17
Alaska	unspecified	17
Arizona	8	17
Arkansas	10	17
California	unspecified	17
Colorado	10	17
Connecticut	unspecified	15
Delaware	unspecified	17
District of Columbia	unspecified	17
Florida	unspecified	17
Georgia	unspecified	16
Hawaii	unspecified	17
Idaho	unspecified	17
Illinois[*]	unspecified	16
Indiana	unspecified	17
Iowa	unspecified	17

STATE	MINIMUM AGE	MAXIMUM AGE
Kansas	10	17
Kentucky	unspecified	17
Louisiana	10	16
Maine	unspecified	17
Maryland	7	17
Massachusetts	7	16
Michigan	unspecified	16
Minnesota	10	17
Mississippi	10	17
Missouri	unspecified	16
Montana	unspecified	17
Nebraska	unspecified	17
Nevada	unspecified	17
New Hampshire	unspecified	16
New Jersey	unspecified	17
New Mexico	unspecified	17
New York	7	15
North Carolina	6	15
North Dakota	unspecified	17
Ohio	unspecified	17
Oklahoma	unspecified	17
Oregon	unspecified	17
Pennsylvania	10	17
Rhode Island	unspecified	17
South Carolina	unspecified	16
South Dakota	10	17
Tennessee	unspecified	17
Texas	10	16
Utah	unspecified	17

STATE	MINIMUM AGE	MAXIMUM AGE
Vermont	10	17
Virginia	unspecified	17
Washington	unspecified	17
West Virginia	unspecified	17
Wisconsin	10	16
Wyoming	unspecified	17

Source: National Center for Juvenile Justice, 2000

APPENDIX 2:
STATES WITH JUDICIAL
WAIVER PROVISIONS

STATE	DISCRETIONARY	PRESUMPTIVE	MANDATORY
Alabama	yes	no	no
Alaska	yes	yes	no
Arizona	yes	yes	no
Arkansas	yes	no	no
California	yes	yes	no
Colorado	yes	yes	no
Connecticut	no	no	yes
Delaware	yes	no	yes
District of Columbia	yes	yes	no
Florida	yes	no	no
Georgia	yes	no	yes
Hawaii	yes	no	no
Idaho	yes	no	no
Illinois	yes	yes	yes
Indiana	yes	no	yes
Iowa	yes	no	no
Kansas	yes	yes	no
Kentucky	yes	no	yes

STATE	DISCRETIONARY	PRESUMPTIVE	MANDATORY
Louisiana	yes	no	yes
Maine	yes	yes	no
Maryland	yes	no	no
Michigan	yes	no	no
Minnesota	yes	yes	no
Mississippi	yes	no	no
Missouri	yes	no	no
Montana	yes	no	no
Nevada	yes	yes	no
New Hampshire	yes	yes	no
New Jersey	yes	yes	yes
North Carolina	yes	no	yes
North Dakota	yes	yes	yes
Ohio	yes	no	yes
Oklahoma	yes	no	no
Oregon	yes	no	no
Pennsylvania	yes	yes	no
Rhode Island	yes	yes	yes
South Carolina	yes	no	yes
South Dakota	yes	no	no
Tennessee	yes	no	no
Texas	yes	no	no
Utah	yes	yes	no
Vermont	yes	no	no
Virginia	yes	no	yes
Washington	yes	no	no
West Virginia	yes	no	yes
Wisconsin	yes	no	no
Wyoming	yes	no	no

Source: National Center for Juvenile Justice, 2000

APPENDIX 3:
STATES WITH PROSECUTORIAL
DISCRETION PROVISIONS

Arizona	Massachusetts
Arkansas	Michigan
California	Montana
Colorado	Nebraska
District of Columbia	Oklahoma
Florida	Vermont
Georgia	Virginia
Louisiana	Wyoming

Source: National Center for Juvenile Justice, 2000

APPENDIX 4:
STATES WITH STATUTORY
EXCLUSION PROVISIONS

Alabama	Mississippi
Alaska	Montana
Arizona	Nevada
California	New Mexico
Delaware	New York
Florida	Oklahoma
Georgia	Oregon
Idaho	Pennsylvania
Illinois	South Carolina
Indiana	South Dakota
Iowa	Utah
Louisiana	Vermont
Maryland	Washington
Massachusetts	Wisconsin
Minnesota	

Source: National Center for Juvenile Justice, 2000

APPENDIX 5:
STATE MINIMUM AGE REQUIREMENTS FOR TRANSFER

STATE	MINIMUM AGE PROVISION
Alabama	14
Alaska	none
Arizona	none
Arkansas	14
California	14
Colorado	12
Connecticut	14
Delaware	none
District of Columbia	none
Florida	none
Georgia	none
Hawaii	none
Idaho	none
Illinois	13
Indiana	none
Iowa	14
Kansas	10

STATE	MINIMUM AGE PROVISION
Kentucky	14
Louisiana	14
Maine	none
Maryland	none
Massachusetts	14
Michigan	14
Minnesota	14
Mississippi	13
Missouri	12
Montana	12
Nebraska	none
Nevada	none
New Hampshire	13
New Jersey	14
New Mexico	15
New York	13
North Carolina	13
North dakota	14
Ohio	14
Oklahoma	none
Oregon	none
Pennsylvania	none
Rhode Island	none
Soth Carolina	none
South Dakota	none
Tennessee	none
Texas	14
Utah	14
Vermont	10

STATE	MINIMUM AGE PROVISION
Virginia	14
Washington	none
West Virginia	none
Wisconsin	none
Wyoming	13

Source: National Center for Juvenile Justice, 2000

APPENDIX 6:
STATES WITH REVERSE
WAIVER PROVISIONS

Arizona	Nevada
Arizona	New York
Arkansas	Oklahoma
Colorado	Oregon
Connecticut	Pennsylvania
Delaware	South Carolina
Georgia	South Dakota
Iowa	Tennessee
Kentucky	Vermont
Maryland	Virginia
Mississippi	Wisconsin
Montana	Wyoming
Nebraska	

Source: National Center for Juvenile Justice, 2000

APPENDIX 7:
STATES WITH AUTOMATIC TRANSFER PROVISIONS FOR JUVENILES PREVIOUSLY PROSECUTED AS ADULTS

Alabama	Missouri
Arizona	Nevada
California	New Hampshire
Delaware	North Carolina
District of Columbia	North Dakota
Florida	Ohio
Hawaii	Oklahoma
Idaho	Oregon
Illinois	Pennsylvania
Indiana	Rhode Island
Iowa	South Dakota
Kansas	Tennessee
Maine	Texas
Maryland	Utah
Michigan	Virginia
Minnesota	Washington
Mississippi	Wisconsin

Source: National Center for Juvenile Justice, 2000

APPENDIX 8:
STATES WITH TRANSFER PROVISIONS
FOR NONVIOLENT OFFENSES

STATE	COVERED OFFENSES
Alabama	Drug offense, any criminal offense
Alaska	Any criminal offense, property offense
Arizona	Any felony, aggravated driving under the influence
Arkansas	Any felony, escape, soliciting a minor to join a gang
California	Drug offense, any criminal offense, property offense
Colorado	Any felony, property offense
Delaware	Drug offense, any criminal offense, property offense
District of Columbia	Any criminal offense, any felony, property offense
Florida	Any criminal offense, property offense, auto theft
Georgia	Any criminal offense, property offense
Hawaii	Any felony
Idaho	Drug offense, any criminal offense, property offense
Illinois	Drug offense, any criminal offense, escape
Iowa	Drug offense
Kansas	Drug offense, any criminal offense
Louisiana	Drug offense, property offense
Michigan	Drug offense, any criminal offense, any felony, property offense, escape

STATE	COVERED OFFENSES
Minnesota	Any felony
Mississippi	Any criminal offense
Missouri	Any felony
Montana	Drug offense, property offense, escape
Nebraska	Any criminal offense, any felony
Nevada	Any criminal offense, any felony
New Hampshire	Any felony
New Jersey	Drug offense, property offense, auto theft
New York	Property offense
North Carolina	Any felony
North Dakota	Drug offense, any criminal offense
Ohio	Any felony, property offense
Oklahoma	Any felony, property offense
Oregon	Property offense, escape
Pennsylvania	Any felony
Rhode Island	Any felony
South Carolina	Drug offense, any criminal offense
South Dakota	Any felony
Tennessee	Any criminal offense
Texas	Drug offense, perjury
Utah	Any felony, property offense
Vermont	Any criminal offense, property offense
Virginia	Any felony
Washington	Any criminal offense, property offense
West Virginia	Drug offense, property offense, treason
Wisconsin	Drug offense, any criminal offense, property offense
Wyoming	Any criminal offense

Source: National Center for Juvenile Justice, 2000

APPENDIX 9:
SUMMARY OF STATE LIMITATIONS ON CONFIDENTIALITY OF JUVENILE COURT PROCEEDINGS AND RECORDS FOR SERIOUS AND VIOLENT JUVENILE OFFENDERS

STATE	OPEN HEARING	RELEASE OF NAME	RELEASE OF RECORDS
Alabama	no	no	yes
Alaska	yes	yes	yes
Arizona	yes	yes	yes
Arkansas	no	yes	yes
California	yes	yes	yes
Colorado	yes	yes	yes
Connecticut	no	no	yes
Delaware	yes	yes	yes
District of Columbia	no	no	yes
Florida	yes	yes	yes
Georgia	yes	yes	yes

STATE	OPEN HEARING	RELEASE OF NAME	RELEASE OF RECORDS
Hawaii	yes	yes	yes
Idaho	yes	yes	yes
Illinois	no	yes	yes
Indiana	yes	yes	yes
Iowa	yes	yes	yes
Kansas	yes	yes	yes
Kentucky	no	yes	yes
Louisiana	yes	yes	yes
Maine	yes	yes	yes
Maryland	yes	no	yes
Michigan	yes	yes	yes
Minnesota	yes	yes	yes
Mississippi	no	yes	yes
Missouri	yes	yes	yes
Montana	yes	yes	yes
Nebraska	no	yes	yes
Nevada	yes	yes	yes
New Hampshire	no	yes	yes
New Jersey	no	yes	yes
New Mexico	yes	no	no
New York	yes	yes	no
North Carolina	no	no	yes
North Dakota	no	yes	yes
Ohio	no	no	no
Oklahoma	yes	yes	yes
Oregon	no	yes	yes
Pennsylvania	yes	yes	yes
Rhode Island	no	yes	yes

STATE	OPEN HEARING	RELEASE OF NAME	RELEASE OF RECORDS
South Carolina	no	yes	yes
South Dakota	yes	yes	yes
Tennessee	no	yes	yes
Texas	yes	yes	yes
Utah	yes	yes	yes
Vermont	no	no	no
Virginia	yes	yes	yes
Washington	yes	yes	yes
West Virginia	no	yes	yes
Wisconsin	yes	yes	yes
Wyoming	no	yes	yes

Source: National Center for Juvenile Justice, 2000

APPENDIX 10:
JUVENILE JUSTICE POPULATION BY AGE AND GENDER AS OF 1999

AGES	TOTAL	MALE	FEMALE
All Ages	272,690,813	133,276,559,	139,414,254
0 to 17	70,199,158	35,960,401	34,238,757
10 to 17	31,310,270	16,069,769	15,240,501
10 to	29,373,373	15,073,594	14,299,779
0 to 5	22,836,804	11,676,463	11,160,341
6 to 9	16,052,084	8,214,169	7,837,915
10 to 12	11,778,325	6,030,404	5,747,921
13 to 14	7,770,159	3,981,303	3,788,856
15	3,820,648	1,962,193	1,858,455
16	3,923,852	2,021,666	1,902,186
17	4,017,286	2,074,203	1,943,083
18 to 20	11,884,287	6,091,438	5,792,849
21 to 24	14,127,439	7,184,549	6,942,890

Source: http://www.ojjdp.ncjrs.org/ojstatbb/ezapop

APPENDIX 11:
STATES WITH BLENDED
SENTENCING PROVISIONS FOR
SERIOUS JUVENILE OFFENDERS

Alaska	Michigan
Arkansas	Minnesota
California	Missouri
Colorado	New Mexico
Connecticut	Oklahoma
Florida	Rhode Island
Idaho	South Carolina
Illinois	Texas
Iowa	Vermont
Kansas	Virginia
Massachusetts	West Virginia

Source: National Center for Juvenile Justice, 2000

APPENDIX 12:
STATE SUBSTANCE ABUSE
RESOURCE DIRECTORY

STATE	AGENCY	TELEPHONE NUMBER
Alabama	Department of Mental Helath	205-271-9253
Alaska	Department of Health and Social Services	907-586-6201
Arizona	Department of Health Services	602-255-1238
Arkansas	Department of Human Services	501-371-2603
California	Department of Alcohol and Drug Abuse	916-445-1940
Colorado	Department of Health	303-320-6137
Connecticut	Alcohol and Drug Abuse Commission	203-566-4145
Delaware	Division of Mental health	302-421-6101
District of Columbia	Department of Human Services	202-724-5641
Florida	Department of Health and Rehabilitative Services	904-488-0396
Georgia	Department of Human Resources	404-894-4785
Hawaii	Department of Health	808-548-4280
Idaho	Idaho Department of Health & Welfare	208-334-4368
Illinois	Department of Mental health	312-793-2907

STATE	AGENCY	TELEPHONE NUMBER
Indiana	Department of Mental health	317-232-7816
Iowa	Department of Substance Abuse	515-281-3641
Kansas	Department of Social Rehabilitation	913-296-3925
Kentucky	Department of Health Services	502-564-2880
Louisiana	Department of Health and Human Services	504-342-2565
Maine	Department of Human Services	207-289-2781
Maryland	State Health Department	301-383-3312
Massachusetts	Department of Public Health	617-727-8617
Michigan	Department of Public Health	517-373-8603
Minnesota	Department of Public Welfare	612-296-4614
Mississippi	Deaprtment of Mental Health	601-359-1297
Missouri	Department of Mental Health	314-751-4942
Montana	Department of Institutions	406-449-2827
Nebraska	Department of Public Institutions	402-471-2851
Nevada	Department of Human Resources	702-885-4790
New Hampshire	Department of Health and Welfare	603-271-4627
New Jersey	Department of Health	609-292-8949
New Mexico	Health and Environment Department	505-984-0020
New York	Division of Substance Abuse Services	518-457-7629
North Carolina	Department of Human Resources	919-733-4670
North Dakota	Department of Human Services	701-224-2767
Ohio	Department of Mental Health	614-466-9023
Oklahoma	Department of Mental Health	405-521-0044
Oregon	Deaprtment of Human Resources	503-378-2163
Pennsylvania	Department of Health	717-787-9857

STATE	AGENCY	TELEPHONE NUMBER
Rhode Island	Department of Mental Health	401-464-2091
South Carolina	Commission on Alcohol and Drug Abuse	803-758-2521
South Dakota	Department of Health	605-773-4806
Tennessee	Department of Mental health	615-741-1921
Texas	Department of Community Affairs	512-443-4100
Utah	Department of Social Services	801-533-6532
Vermont	Agency of Human Resources	802-241-2170
Virginia	Department of Mental Health	804-786-5313
Washington	Department of Social and Health Services	206-753-5866
West Virginia	Department of Health	304-348-2276
Wisconsin	Department of Health and Social Services	608-266-2717
Wyoming	Alcohol and Drug Abuse Programs	307-777-7115

APPENDIX 13:
NEW YORK STATE PENAL LAW SEXUAL ABUSE PROVISIONS

§ 130.65—Sexual Abuse in the First Degree

A person is guilty of sexual abuse in the first degree when he subjects another person to sexual contact:

1. By forcible compulsion; or

2. When the other person is incapable of consent by reason of being physically helpless; or

3. When the other person is less than eleven years old.

Sexual abuse in the first degree is a class D felony.

§ 130.60—Sexual Abuse in the Second Degree

A person is guilty of sexual abuse in the second degree when he subjects another person to sexual contact and when such other person is:

1. Incapable of consent by reason of some factor other than being less than seventeen years old; or

2. Less than fourteen years old.

Sexual abuse in the second degree is a class A misdemeanor.

§ 130.55—Sexual Abuse in the Third Degree

A person is guilty of sexual abuse in the third degree when he subjects another person to sexual contact without the latter's consent; exept that in any prosecution under this section, it is an affirmative defense that (a) such other person's lack of consent was due solely to incapacity to consent by reason of being less than seventeen years old, and (b) such other person was more than fourteen years old, and (c) the defendant was less than five years older than such other person.

Sexual abuse in the third degree is a class B misdemeanor.

APPENDIX 14:
NEW YORK STATE PENAL LAW
RAPE PROVISIONS

§ 130.35—Rape in the First Degree

A male is guilty of rape in the first degree when he engages in sexual intercourse with a female:

    1. By forcible compulsion; or

    2. Who is incapable of consent by reason of being physically helpless; or

    3. Who is less than eleven years old.

Rape in the first degree is a class B felony.

§ 130.30—Rape in the Second Degree

A person is guilty of rape in the second degree when, being eighteen years old or more, he or she engages in sexual intercourse with another person to whom the actor is not married less than fourteen years old.

Rape in the second degree is a class D felony.

§ 130.25—Rape in the Third Degree

A person is guilty of rape in the third degree when:

    1. He or she engages in sexual intercourse with another person to whom the actor is not married who is incapable of consent by reason of some factor other than being less than seventeen years old; or

    2. Being twenty-one years old or more, he or she engages in sexual intercourse with another person to whom the actor is not married less than seventeen years old.

Sexual abuse in the third degree is a class E felony.

APPENDIX 15:
STATE STATUTORY RAPE LAWS

STATE	VICTIM UNDER AGE	OFFENDER OVER AGE	NOTES	APPLICABLE STATUTE
Alabama	12	not specified	if victim over 12 to16 offender must be over 16	Alabama Code Ann. §§13-1-133
Alaska	16	16		Alaska Statutes Ann. §11.15.120
Arizona	18	not specified		Arizona Rev. Statutes Ann. §13-1405
Arkansas	11	not specified	if victim over 11 to14 offender must be over 18	Arkansas Rev. Statutes Ann. §§41-1803
California	18	not specified		California Ann. Code; Penal Code §161.5
Colorado	15	4 years older		Colorado Rev. Statutes §§18-3-404
Connecticut	15	not specified		Connecticut Gen. Statutes Ann. §53a-71

STATE	VICTIM UNDER AGE	OFFENDER OVER AGE	NOTES	APPLICABLE STATUTE
Delaware	16	not specified		Delaware Code Ann. §11-767
District of Columbia	16	not specified		District of Columbia Rev. Code §22-2801
Florida	11	not specified		Florida Statutes Ann. §749.011
Georgia	14	not specified		Georgia Code Ann. §26-2001
Idaho	18	not specified	if offender is under 14 physical ability must be proven for conviction	Idaho Code Ann. §18-6101
Illinois	16	17		Illinois Statutes Ann. §38-11-4
Indiana	12	not specified	if victim over 12 to 16 offender must be over 16	Indiana Statutes Ann. §35-42-4-3
Iowa	14	6 years older		Iowa Code Ann. §21-3503
Kansas	16	not specified		Kansas Statutes Ann. §14:43
Kentucky	16	not specified		Kentucky Rev. Statutes §510.040
Louisiana	17	17		Louisiana Statutes Ann. §14:43
Maine	14	3 years older	if victim 16 offender must be 5 years older	Maine Rev. Statutes Ann. §§17A-254

STATE	VICTIM UNDER AGE	OFFENDER OVER AGE	NOTES	APPLICABLE STATUTE
Maryland	16	4 years older		Maryland Code Ann. §§27-463
Massachusetts	16	not specified		Massachusetts Gen. Laws Ann. §§265-22A
Michigan	16	not specified		Michigan Compiled Laws Ann. §28.788
Minnesota	13	3 years older	if victim 13 to 16 offender must be 4 years older	Minnesota Statutes Ann. §§609.342
Mississippi	18	not specified		Mississippi Code Ann. §§97-3-65
Missouri	16	not specified		Missouri Ann. Statutes §§566.030
Montana	16	3 years older		Montana Code Ann. §94-5-502
Nebraska	18	18		Nebraska Rev. Statutes §28.408.03
Nevada	16	18		Nevada Rev. Statutes §§200.364
New Hampshire	16	not specified		New Hampshire Rev. Statutes Ann. §632-A-4
New Jersey	13	not specified	if victim is 13 to 16 offender must be 4 years older	New Jersey Statutes Ann. §2C:14-2
New Mexico	18	not specified		New Mexico Statutes Ann. §§30-9-11

STATE	VICTIM UNDER AGE	OFFENDER OVER AGE	NOTES	APPLICABLE STATUTE
New York	11	not specified	if victim is 14 to 17 offender must be over 18	New York Consolidated Laws; Penal Code §§130.35
North Carolina	12	4 years older		North Carolina Gen. Statutes Ann. §§14-27-2
North Dakota	minor	adult		North Dakota Century Code Ann. §§12.1-20-03
Ohio	15	not specified		Ohio Rev. Code §§2907.02
Oklahoma	14	18		Oklahoma Statutes Ann. §§21-1111
Oregon	18	18		Oregon Rev. Statutes §§163.355
Pennsylvania	14	18		Pennsylvania Statutes Ann. §18-3122
Rhode Island	16	not specified		Rhode Island Gen. Laws Ann. §§22-22-1
South Carolina	14	3 years older		South Carolina Code Ann. §16-3-655
South Dakota	16	not specified		South Dakota Compiled Laws Ann. §§22-22-1
Tennessee	16	18		Tennessee Code Ann. §§39-3703

STATE	VICTIM UNDER AGE	OFFENDER OVER AGE	NOTES	APPLICABLE STATUTE
Texas	17	not specified		Texas Statutes Ann.; Penal Code §21.09
Utah	16	not specified		Utah Code Ann. §§76-5-401
Vermont	16	not specified		Vermont Statutes Ann. §13-3252
Virginia	15	not specified		Virginia Code Ann. §§18.2-61
Washington	16	2 years older		Washington Rev. Code Ann. §§9A.44.070
West Virginia	11	14	if victim is 11 to 16 offender must be 4 years older	West Virginia Code Ann. §§61-8B-3
Wisconsin	18	not specified		Wisconsin Statutes Ann.
Wyoming	16	4 years older		Wyoming Statutes Ann. §§6-63.4

APPENDIX 16:
NATIONAL CHILD ABUSE AND NEGLECT DATA SYSTEM—CHILD MALTREATMENT DATA—1997

AGE	PERCENTAGE OF VICTIMS
Under 1	7%
1-5	31%
6-10	30%
11-15	23%
Over 16	6%
Unknown	3%
RACE/ETHNICITY	**PERCENTAGE OF VICTIMS**
Alaska Native/Aleutian	2%
Asian/Pacific Islander	1%
Black	29%
Hispanic	8%
White	58%
Other	2%
Unable to Determine	8%

Note: Percentages may total more than 100 percent because Hispanics may be counted both by Hispanic ethnicity and by race.

MALTREATMENT TYPE	PERCENTAGE OF VICTIMS
Emotional Abuse	4%
Medical Neglect	3%
Neglect	56%
Physical Abuse	20%
Sexual Abuse	12%
Other	19%
Unknown	0%

Note: Percentages may total more than 100 percent because children could have been victims of more than one type of maltreatment.

Source: United States Department of Health and Human Services, National Child Abuse and Neglect Data System (NCANDS), 1997.

APPENDIX 17:
AGE WHERE CONSENT
REQUIRED FOR ADOPTION

STATE	AGE CONSENT REQUIRED	APPLICABLE STATUTE
Alabama	14	Alabama Code Ann. §26-10-3
Alaska	10	Alaska Statutes Ann. §20.15.040
Arizona	12	Arizona Rev. Statutes Ann. §8-106
Arkansas	10	Arkansas Rev. Statutes Ann. §56-206
California	12	California Ann. Codes; Civil Code §225
Colorado	12	Colorado Rev. Statutes §19-4-107
Connecticut	14	Connecticut general. Statutes Ann. §45-61
Delaware	14	Delaware Code Ann. §45-61
District of Columbia	14	District of Columbia Rev. Code §16-304
Florida	12	Florida Statutes Ann. §63.062
Georgia	14	Georgia Code Ann. §74.403
Hawaii	10	Hawaii Rev. Laws §578-2
Idaho	12	Idaho Code Ann. §16-1505
Illinois	14	Illinois Statutes Ann. §4-9.1-12
Indiana	14	Indiana Statutes Ann. §31-3-1-6

STATE	AGE CONSENT REQUIRED	APPLICABLE STATUTE
Iowa	14	Iowa Code Ann. §600.7
Kansas	14	Kansas Statutes Ann. §59.2102
Kentucky	12	Kentucky Rev. Statutes §199.500
Louisiana	Not specified	Louisiana Statutes Ann. §9-422.1
Maine	14	Maine Rev. Statutes Ann. §19-532
Maryland	10	Maryland Code Ann. §16-74
Massachusetts	12	Massachusetts general. Laws Ann. §210-2
Michigan	10	Michigan Compiled Laws Ann. §710.43
Minnesota	14	Minnesota Statutes Ann. §259.24
Mississippi	14	Missouri Ann. Statutes §93-17-5
Missouri	14	Missouri Ann. Statutes §543.030
Montana	Not specified	Montana Code Ann. §61-205
Nebraska	14	Nebraska Rev. Statutes §43.104
Nevada	14	Nevada Rev. Statutes §127.020
New Hampshire	12	New Hampshire Statutes Ann. §170-B:5
New Jersey	At 10 desire will be considered	New Jersey Statutes Ann. §9.3-49
New Mexico	10	New Mexico Statutes Ann. §40-7-6
New York	14	New York Consolidated Laws; Domestic Relations Law §111
North Carolina	12	North Carolina general. Statutes Ann. §48-10
North Dakota	10	North Dakota Century Code Ann. §14-15-05
Ohio	12	Ohio Rev. Code §3107.06
Oklahoma	12	Oklahoma Statutes Ann. §10-60.11
Oregon	14	Oregon Rev. Statutes §109.328
Pennsylvania	12	Pennsylvania Statutes Ann. §1-411
Rhode Island	14	Rhode Island general. Laws Ann. §15-7-5
South Carolina	Not specified	South Carolina Code Ann. §15-45-50

STATE	AGE CONSENT REQUIRED	APPLICABLE STATUTE
South Dakota	12	South Dakota Compiled Laws Ann. §15-45-50
Tennessee	14	Tennessee Code Ann. §36-115
Texas	14	Texas Statutes Ann.; Civil Statutes Art. 46a.-6
Utah	12	Utah Code Ann. §78-30-6
Vermont	Not specified	Vermont Statutes Ann. §15-435
Virginia	14	Virginia Code Ann. §63.1-225
Washington	14	Washington Rev. Code Ann. §26.32.030
West Virginia	12	West Virginia Code Ann. §48-4-1
Wisconsin	14	Wisconsin Statutes Ann. §48-84

APPENDIX 18:
STATE MAXIMUM COMPULSORY
EDUCATION AGE REQUIREMENT

STATE	AGE REQUIREMENT	APPLICABLE STATUTE
Alabama	16	Alabama Code Ann. §16-28-1
Alaska	16	Alaska Statutes Ann. § 14.30.010
Arizona	16	Arizona Rev. Statutes Ann. §§15-301
Arkansas	16	Arkansas Rev. Statutes Ann. §80-1501
California	16	California Ann. Codes; Education §§48200
Colorado	16	Colorado Rev. Statutes §§22-33-101
Connecticut	16	Connecticut general. Statutes Ann. §§10-184
Delaware	16	Delaware Code Ann. §§14-2701
District of Columbia	16	District of Columbia Rev. Code §§31-201
Florida	16	Florida Statutes Ann. §§232.01
Georgia	16	Georgia Code Ann. §§32-2101
Hawaii	18	Hawaii Rev. Laws §§298-1
Idaho	16	Idaho Code Ann. §§33-201

STATE	AGE REQUIREMENT	APPLICABLE STATUTE
Illinois	16	Illinois Statutes Ann. §§26-1
Indiana	16	Indiana Statutes Ann. §§20-8.1-3-1
Iowa	16	Iowa Code Ann. §§282.1
Kansas	16	Kansas Statutes Ann. §§72-1101
Kentucky	16	Kentucky Rev. Statutes §§158.010
Louisiana	16	Louisiana Statutes Ann. §§R.S. 17:221
Maine	17	Main Rev. Statutes Ann. Title 20 §§811
Maryland	16	Maryland Code Ann. §7-301; §4-120
Massachusetts	16	Massachusetts general. Laws Ann. §§76-1
Michigan	16	Michigan Compiled Laws Ann. §§380.1561
Minnesota	16	Minnesota Statutes Ann. §§120.06
Mississippi	13	Mississippi Code Ann. §§37-13-91
Missouri	16	Missouri Ann. Statues §§167.011
Montana	16	Montana Code Ann. §§75-6301
Nebraska	16	Nebraska Rev. Statutes §79-201.01
Nevada	17	Nevada Rev. Statutes Title 34 §§392.040
New Hampshire	16	New Hampshire Rev. Statutes Ann. §§193:1
New Jersey	16	New Jersey Statutes Ann. §§18A:38-1
New Mexico	16	New Mexico Statutes Ann. §§22-12-1
New York	16	New York Consolidated Laws; Education Law §§3201
North Carolina	16	North Carolina Gen. Statutes Ann.; Article 20 §§115

STATE	AGE REQUIREMENT	APPLICABLE STATUTE
North Dakota	16	North Dakota Century Code Ann. §§15-34.01
Ohio	18	Ohio Rev. Code §§3321.01
Oklahoma	18	Oklahoma Statutes Ann. §§70-10-105
Oregon	18	Oregon Rev. Statutes §§339.005
Pennsylvania	17	Pennsylvania Statutes Ann.; Title 24 §§13-1301
Rhode Island	16	Rhode Island general. Laws Ann. §§16-19-1
South Carolina	16	South Carolina Code Ann. §§59-65-10
South Dakota	16	South Dakota Compiled Laws Ann. §§13-27-1
Tennessee	16	Tennessee Code Ann. §§21.031
Texas	17	Texas Statutes Ann. §§21.031
Utah	18	Utah Code Ann. §§53-24-1
Vermont	16	Vermont Statutes Ann.
Virginia	17	Virginia Code Ann. §§22-2751.1
Washington	15	Washington Rev. Code Ann. §§28A.27.010
West Virginia	16	West Virginia Code Ann. §§18-8-1
Wisconsin	16	Wisconsin Statutes Ann. §§118.15
Wyoming	16	Wyoming Statutes Ann. §§21-4-101

APPENDIX 19:
AGE OF MAJORITY BY STATE

STATE	AGE
Alabama	19
Alaska	18
Arizona	18
Arkansas	18
California	18
Colorado	18
Connecticut	18
Delaware	18
District of Columbia	18
Florida	18
Georgia	18
Hawaii	18
Idaho	18
Illinois	18
Indiana	18
Iowa	18
Kansas	18
Kentucky	18

STATE	AGE
Louisiana	18
Maine	18
Maryland	18
Massachusetts	18
Michigan	18
Minnesota	18
Mississippi	21
Missouri	18
MontanA	18
Nebraska	19
Nevada	18
New Hampshire	18
New Jersey	18
New Mexico	18
New York	18
North Carolina	18
North Dakota	18
Ohio	18
Oklahoma	18
Oregon	18
Pennsylvania	21
Rhode Island	18
South Carolina	18
South Dakota	18
Tennessee	18
Texas	18
Utah	18
Vermont	18
Virginia	18

STATE	AGE
Washington	18
West Virginia	18
Wisconsin	18
Wyoming	18

APPENDIX 20:
STATE EMANCIPATION STATUTES

STATE	STATUTE	ADDITIONAL PROVISIONS
Alabama	Relief of Minor Children from Disabilities of Nonage, Title 26, Chapter 13	Only available to minors over age of 18
Alaska	none	none
Arizona	none	none
Arkansas	none	none
California	Emancipation of Minors Law, Family Code §§ 7000-7002	none
Colorado	Emancipated Juvenile, Title 19, Article 1	none
Connecticut	Order of Emancipation, Title 46b-150	none
Delaware	none	none
District of Columbia	none	none
Florida	Removal of Disabilities of Nonage, Chapter 743	Must be at least 16 years of age and have a petition filed by natural or legal guardian or guardian ad litem
Georgia	none	none
Hawaii	Emancipation, Chapter 577-25, Division 3, Title 31	none

STATE	STATUTE	ADDITIONAL PROVISIONS
Idaho	none	none
Illinois	Emancipation of Mature Minors Act, Chapter 750, ILCS 30	Must be at least 16 years old
Indiana	none	none
Iowa	none	none
Kansas	District Court May Confer Rights of Majority, Chapter 38, Article 108	none
Kentucky	none	none
Louisiana	Emancipation, Civil Code §365, Chapter 2 et seq.	none
Maine	none	none
Maryland	Emancipation, Family Law Code 3-826.1	none
Massachusetts	Emancipation, Chapter 201, §5	none
Michigan	Emancipation of Minors Act, Chapter 722.4	none
Minnesota	none	none
Mississippi	none	none
Missouri	none	none
Montana	Emancipation, Title 41, Chapter 3, Part 4	none
Nebraska	none	none
Nevada	Emancipation, Title 11, Chapter 129	none
New Hampshire	Emancipation, Title 1, Chapter 21-B-2	none
New Jersey	none	none
New Mexico	Emancipation, Chapter 32A, Article 21	none
New York	none	none
North Carolina	Emancipation, Chapter 7B, Sub-chapter 4, Article 35	none

STATE	STATUTE	ADDITIONAL PROVISIONS
North Dakota	none	none
Ohio	none	none
Oklahoma	Confirmation of Majority Rights	Gives minors the legal right to contract but rarely granted in court
Oregon	Emancipation, Chapter 419B	none
Pennsylvania	Laws vary according to county	Check local law
Rhode Island	Emancipation, Title 14, Chapter 1-59.1	
South Carolina	none	none
South Dakota	Emancipation, Title 25, Chapter 25-5-18 through 27	none
Tennessee	none	none
Texas	none	none
Utah	none	none
Vermont	Emancipation, Title 12, Part 10, Chapter 17	none
Virginia	Emancipation, Title 16.1-331	
Washington	Emancipation, Revised Code of Washington §13.64	none
West Virginia	Emancipation, Chapter 49, Article 7-27	none
Wisconsin	none	none
Wyoming	Emancipation, Title 14, Chapter 1, Article 2	

Source: National Center for Juvenile Justice, 2000

APPENDIX 21:
STATE MINIMUM AGE REQUIREMENTS
FOR MARRIAGE

STATE	AGE WITH PARENTAL CONSENT		AGE WITHOUT PARENTAL CONSENT	
	Male	Female	Male	Female
Alabama	14	14	18	18
Alaska	16	16	18	18
Arizona	16	16	18	18
Arkansas	17	16	18	18
California	None		None	18
Colorado	16	16	18	18
Connecticut	16	16	18	18
Delaware	18	16	18	18
District of Columbia	16	16	18	18
Florida	16	16	18	18
Georgia	None	None	16	16
Hawaii	16	16	18	18
Idaho	16	16	18	18
Illinois	16	16	18	18
Indiana	17	17	18	18
Iowa	16	16	18	18

STATE	AGE WITH PARENTAL CONSENT		AGE WITHOUT PARENTAL CONSENT	
	Male	Female	Male	Female
Kansas	Under 18	Under18	18	18
Kentucky	None	None	18	18
Louisiana	18	18	18	18
Maine	16	16	18	18
Maryland	16	16	18	18
Massachusetts	16	16	18	18
Michigan	16	16	18	18
Minnesota	16	16	18	18
Mississippi	None	None	17	15
Missouri	15	15	18	18
Montana	16	16	18	18
Nebraska	17	17	17	17
Nevada	16	16	18	18
New Hampshire	14	13	18	18
New Jersey	16	16	18	18
New Mexico	16	16	18	18
New York	16	16	18	18
North Carolina	16	16	18	18
North Dakota	16	16	18	18
Ohio	18	16	18	18
Oklahoma	16	16	18	18
Oregon	17	17	18	18
Pennsylvania	16	16	18	18
Rhode Island	18	16	18	18
South Carolina	16	14	18	18
South Dakota	16	16	18	18
Tennessee	16	16	18	18

STATE	AGE WITH PARENTAL CONSENT		AGE WITHOUT PARENTAL CONSENT	
	Male	Female	Male	Female
Texas	14	14	18	18
Utah	14	14	18	18
Vermont	16	16	18	18
Virginia	16	16	18	18
Washington	17	17	18	18
West Virginia	18	18	18	18
Wisconsin	16	16	18	18
Wyoming	16	16	18	18

In Alabama, Florida, Virginia and the District of Columbia, parental consent is not required if the minor was previously married.

In Alaska, Arkansas, Delaware, Florida, Indiana, Kentucky, Maryland, Michigan, New Jersey, New Mexico, North Carolina, Ohio, Oklahoma, Puerto Rico, South Carolina, South Dakota, Virginia, and West Virginia, there is a statutory procedure whereby younger parties may obtain a license in case of pregnancy or birth of child.

In Alaska, Arizona, Arkansas, Colorado, Connecticut, Idaho, Iowa, Kansas, Kentucky, Louisiana, Maine, Minnesota, Nevada, New Hampshire, New Jersey, Ohio, Puerto Rico, Vermont, and the Virgin Islands, younger parties may marry with parental consent and permission of the court, or in some cases with judicial consent alone.

In Texas, parental consent and permission of the court is required below age 18.

APPENDIX 22:
STATE MINIMUM AGE REQUIREMENT
FOR EMPLOYMENT

STATE	MINIMUM AGE REQUIREMENT
Alabama	16
Alaska	16
Arizona	14
Arkansas	14
California	15
Colorado	16
Connecticut	16
Delaware	14
District of Columbia	14
Florida	14
Georgia	16
Hawaii	16
Idaho	14
Illinois	16
Indiana	14
Iowa	16
Kansas	14

STATE	MINIMUM AGE REQUIREMENT
Kentucky	16
Louisiana	16
Maine	16
Maryland	16
Massachusetts	16
Michigan	14
Minnesota	14
Mississippi	14
Missouri	14
Montana	16
Nebraska	14
Nevada	14
New Hampshire	16
New Jersey	16
New Mexico	14
New York	16
North Carolina	16
North Dakota	14
Ohio	16
Oklahoma	14
Oregon	14
Pennsylvania	16
Rhode Island	16
South Carolina	16
South Dakota	14
Tennessee	14
Texas	15
Utah	16
Vermont	14

STATE	MINIMUM AGE REQUIREMENT
Virginia	16
Washington	14
West Virginia	16
Wisconsin	16
Wyoming	16

APPENDIX 23:
STATE MINIMUM AGE REQUIREMENT FOR CIGARETTE PURCHASE

STATE	MINIMUM AGE REQUIREMENT
Alabama	19
Alaska	19
Arizona	18
Arkansas	18
California	18
Colorado	18
Connecticut	18
Delaware	18
District of Columbia	18
Florida	18
Georgia	18
Hawaii	18
Idaho	18
Illinois	18
Indiana	18
Iowa	18
Kansas	18

STATE	MINIMUM AGE REQUIREMENT
Kentucky	18
Louisiana	18
Maine	18
Maryland	18
Massachusetts	18
Michigan	18
Minnesota	18
Mississippi	18
Missouri	18
Montana	18
Nebraska	18
Nevada	18
New Hampshire	18
New Jersey	18
New Mexico	18
New York	18
North Carolina	18
North Dakota	18
Ohio	18
Oklahoma	18
oregon	18
Pennsylvania	18
Rhode island	18
South Carolina	18
South Dakota	18
Tennessee	18
Texas	18
Utah	18
Vermont	18

STATE	MINIMUM AGE REQUIREMENT
Virginia	18
Washington	18
West Virginia	18
Wisconsin	18
Wyoming	18

Source: Center for Disease Control, State Tobacco Activities Tracking and Evaluation System (STATE), 2000.

APPENDIX 24:
STATE YOUNG DRIVERS LAWS

STATE	MINIMUM AGE LEARNER'S PERMIT (LP)	MINIMUM AGE REGULAR LICENSE	LP REQUIRED BEFORE REGULAR LICENSE	MINIMUM LP PERIOD	LP EXPIRATION	NIGHT DRIVING RESTRICTIONS	SEE FOOTNOTE
ALABAMA	15	16	NO	N/A	4 YEARS	NO	N/A
ALASKA	14	16	NO	N/A	2 YEARS	NO	N/A
ARIZONA	15-6MOS	16	NO	N/A	1 YEAR	NO	N/A
ARKANSAS	14	16	YES	30 DAYS	60 DAYS	NO	N/A

STATE	MINIMUM AGE LEARNER'S PERMIT (LP)	MINIMUM AGE REGULAR LICENSE	LP REQUIRED BEFORE REGULAR LICENSE	MINIMUM LP PERIOD	LP EXPIRATION	NIGHT DRIVING RESTRICTIONS	SEE FOOTNOTE
CALIFORNIA	15-6MOS	16	YES	180 DAYS	1 YEAR	MIDNIGHT-5AM UNTIL AGE 17	N/A
COLORADO	15-3MOS	16	YES	90 DAYS	8 MONTHS	NO	N/A
CONNECTICUT	16	16-6MOS	YES	180 DAYS	UNTIL AGE 18	NO	1
DELAWARE	15-10MOS	16	NO	N/A	760 DAYS	NO	N/A
DISTRICT OF COLUMBIA	16	16	YES	N/A	3 MONTHS	NO	N/A
FLORIDA	15	16	YES	180 DAYS	6 YEARS	11PM-6AM AT AGE 16; 1-5 AM AT AGE 17	N/A
GEORGIA	15	16	YES	1 YEAR	2 YEARS	1-5AM UNTIL AGE 18	N/A
HAWAII	15	15	YES	90 DAYS	180 DAYS	NO	N/A
IDAHO	15	15	NO	N/A	180 DAYS	NO	N/A

STATE	MINIMUM AGE LEARNER'S PERMIT (LP)	MINIMUM AGE REGULAR LICENSE	LP REQUIRED BEFORE REGULAR LICENSE	MINIMUM LP PERIOD	LP EXPIRATION	NIGHT DRIVING RESTRICTIONS	SEE FOOTNOTE
ILLINOIS	15	16	YES	90 DAYS	2 YEARS	11PM-6AM FROM MON-THURS AND MIDNIGHT TO 6AM FROM FRIDAY TO SUNDAY UNTIL AGE 17	N/A
INDIANA	15	16-1MO	YES	60 DAYS	UNTIL AGE 16-3MOS	NO	N/A
IOWA	14	16	YES	N/A	2 YEARS FROM BIRTHDAY IN YEAR OF ISSUANCE	NO	N/A
KANSAS	14	16	NO	N/A	1 YEAR	NO	N/A
KENTUCKY	16	16-6MOS	YES	180 DAYS	1 YEAR	NO	N/A
LOUISIANA	15	16	YES	90 DAYS	4 YEARS	11PM-5AM UNTIL AGE 17	N/A
MAINE	15	16	YES	90 DAYS	18 MONTHS	NO	N/A

STATE	MINIMUM AGE LEARNER'S PERMIT (LP)	MINIMUM AGE REGULAR LICENSE	LP REQUIRED BEFORE REGULAR LICENSE	MINIMUM LP PERIOD	LP EXPIRATION	NIGHT DRIVING RESTRICTIONS	SEE FOOTNOTE
MARYLAND	15-9MOS	16	YES	14 DAYS	180 DAYS	MIDNIGHT-5AM FOR 1 YEAR OR UNTIL AGE 18	N/A
MASSACHUSETTS	16	16-6MOS	YES	N/A	1 YEAR	1-4AM UNTIL AGE 18	
MICHIGAN	15	16	YES	180 DAYS	1 YEAR	MIDNIGHT-5AM UNTIL AGE 17	
MINNESOTA	15	16	YES	180 DAYS	1 YEAR	NO	N/A
MISSISSIPPI	15	16	YES	30 DAYS	1 YEAR	NO	N/A
MISSOURI	15-6MOS	16	NO	N/A	6 MONTHS	NO	N/A
MONTANA	14-6MOS	15	NO	N/A	6 MONTHS	NO	N/A
NEBRASKA	15	16	NO	N/A	1 YEAR	NO	N/A
NEVADA	15-6MOS	16	NO	N/A	8 MONTHS	NO	N/A
NEW HAMPSHIRE	16	16-3MOS	YES	90 DAYS	N/A	1-5AM UNTIL AGE 18	
NEW JERSEY	16	17	YES	N/A	1 YEAR-3MOS	NO	N/A

STATE	MINIMUM AGE LEARNER'S PERMIT (LP)	MINIMUM AGE REGULAR LICENSE	LP REQUIRED BEFORE REGULAR LICENSE	MINIMUM LP PERIOD	LP EXPIRATION	NIGHT DRIVING RESTRICTIONS	SEE FOOTNOTE
NEW MEXICO	15	15	YES	N/A	6 MONTHS	NO	N/A
NEW YORK	16	16	YES	N/A	3 YEARS	9PM-5AM UNTIL AGE 18	2
NORTH CAROLINA	15	16	YES	1 YEAR	18 MONTHS	9PM-5AM FOR 6 MONTHS OR UNTIL AGE 18	N/A
NORTH DAKOTA	14	16	YES	90 DAYS	1 YEAR	NO	N/A
OHIO	15-6MOS	16	YES	6 MONTHS	1 YEAR	1AM-5AM UNTIL AGE 17	
OKLAHOMA	15-6MOS	16	NO	N/A	4 YEARS	NO	N/A
OREGON	15	16	NO	N/A	18 MONTHS	NO	N/A
PENNSYLVANIA	16	16	YES	N/A	120 DAYS	MIDNIGHT-5AM UNTIL AGE 18	N/A
RHODE ISLAND	16	16	YES	N/A 180 DAYS	NO	N/A	

STATE	MINIMUM AGE LEARNER'S PERMIT (LP)	MINIMUM AGE REGULAR LICENSE	LP REQUIRED BEFORE REGULAR LICENSE	MINIMUM LP PERIOD	LP EXPIRATION	NIGHT DRIVING RESTRICTIONS	SEE FOOTNOTE
SOUTH CAROLINA	15	15	YES	15 DAYS	12 MONTHS	6PM-6AM EST AND 8PM-6AM EDT UNTIL AGE 16	N/A
SOUTH DAKOTA	14	16	NO	N/A	180 DAYS	NO	4
TENNESSEE	15	16	NO	90 DAYS	1 YEAR	NO	3
TEXAS	15	16	YES	N/A	1 YEAR	NO	N/A
UTAH	16	16	YES	N/A	6 MONTHS	NO	5
VERMONT	15	16	YES	N/A	2 YEARS	NO	N/A
VIRGINIA	15	16	YES	180 DAYS	INDEFINITE	NO	N/A
WASHINGTON	15	16	YES	N/A	1 YEAR	NO	N/A
WEST VIRGINIA	15	16	YES	N/A	UNTIL AGE 16-2MOS	NO	N/A
WISCONSIN	15-6MOS	16	YES	N/A	6 MONTHS	NO	N/A
WYOMING	15	16	NO	10 DAYS	1 YEAR	NO	N/A

NOTES:

1. In Connecticut, the 180-day minimum learner's period is reduced to 120 days for applicants who have completed approved driver education.

2. In New York, licensing laws prohibit people with DJ licenses (16 and 17 year-olds) from driving in New York City.

3. In Tennessee, the 3-month minimum learner's period is waived for applicants who have completed approved driver education.

4. South Dakota issues a restricted license which allows 14 and 15 year-olds to drive unsupervised between the h ours of 6am to 8pm; at other times they are allowed to drive only under the supervision of a parent or guardian. The restricted license becomes a regular license when the holder turns 16.

5. In Utah, instructional permits also are issued to people 15 years and 9 months old. Valid for 1 year, these permit driving only with a professional driving instructor. Instructors may give practice permits, valid for 90 days, that allow driving only with a parent or guardian.[1]

---

[1]   Source: Insurance Institute for Highway Safety.

GLOSSARY

Abortion—The knowing destruction of the life of an unborn child.

Adoption—Legal process pursuant to state statute in which a child's legal rights and duties toward his natural parent(s) are terminated and similar rights and duties toward his adoptive parents are substituted.

Adjudicatory Hearing—The process by which it is determined whether the allegations in a complaint can be proven, and, if so, whether they fall within the jurisdictional categories of the juvenile court.

Banishment—A punishment inflicted upon criminals, by compelling them to leave a country for a specified period of time, or for life. Synonymous with exilement or deportation, importing a compulsory loss of one's country.

Capital Crime—A crime for which the death penalty may, but need not necessarily, be imposed.

Capital Punishment—Punishment by death for capital crimes.

Child Abuse—Any form of cruelty to a child's physical, moral or mental well-being.

Child Custody—The care, control and maintenance of a child which may be awarded by a court to one of the parents of the child.

Child Labor Laws—Network of laws on both federal and state levels prescribing working conditions for children in terms of hours and nature of work which may be performed, all designed to protect the child.

Child Protective Agency—A state agency responsible for the investigation of child abuse and neglect reports.

Child Support—The legal obligation of parents to contribute to the economic maintenance of their children.

Child Welfare—A generic term which embraces the totality of measures necessary for a child's well being; physical, moral and mental.

Common Law—All the statutory and case law background of England and the American colonies before the American revolution.

Compulsory Education—The legal obligation to attend school up to a certain age.

Corporal Punishment—Physical punishment as distinguished from pecuniary punishment or a fine; any kind of punishment of, or inflicted on, the body.

Delinquent—An infant of not more than a specified age who has violated criminal laws or engages in disobedient, indecent or immoral conduct, and is in need of treatment, rehabilitation, or supervision.

Disposition—The process by which the juvenile court decides what is to be done with, for, or about the child who has been found to be within its jurisdiction.

Due Process Rights—All rights which are of such fundamental importance as to require compliance with due process standards of fairness and justice.

Emancipation—The surrender of care, custody and earnings of a child, as well as renunciation of parental duties.

Felony—A crime of a graver or more serious nature than those designated as misdemeanors. Under federal law, and many state statutes, any offense punishable by death or imprisonment for a term exceeding one year.

Forfeiture—The loss of goods or chattels, as a punishment for some crime or misdemeanor in the party forfeiting, and as a compensation for the offense and injury committed against him to whom they are forfeited.

Hallucinogens—Natural and man-made drugs which affect the mind, causing distortions in physical senses and mental reactions.

Hearing—A proceeding with definite issues of fact or law to be tried in which witnesses and parties may be heard.

Incest—Incest is generally recognized as sexual contact between persons who are biologically related or between stepparents and stepchildren.

Infancy—The state of a person who is under the age of legal majority.

Infancy Presumption—At common law, the conclusive presumption that children under the age of seven were without criminal capacity.

Inhalants—Chemicals which emit fumes or vapors which, when inhaled, produce symptoms similar to intoxication.

Juvenile Court—A court which has special jurisdiction, of a parental nature, over delinquent, dependent and neglected children.

Miranda Rights—Warnings which must be given, or waived, prior to any custodial interrogation. Otherwise, no evidence obtained in the interrogation may be used against the accused. In Miranda v. Arizona, the Supreme Court ruled that the following warnings must be given: 1. He has a right to remain silent; 2. Any statement he does make may be used as evidence against him; 3. He has the right to the presence of an attorney; 4. If he cannot afford an attorney, one will be appointed for him prior to any questioning if he so desires.

Narcotics—Generic term for any drug which dulls the senses or induces sleep and which commonly becomes addictive after prolonged use.

Neglect—The failure of a child's parent or custodian, by reason of cruelty, mental incapacity, immorality, or depravity, to provide necessary physical, emotional, medical, surgical, institutional or hospital care for the child, or to otherwise properly care for the child.

Pedophilia—Refers to recurrent, intense, sexual urges, and sexually arousing fantasies, involving sexual activity with a prepubescent child.

Peers—Those who are a man's equals in rank and station.

Reconstituted Family—A family in which the original parent has divorced and remarried.

Selective Emancipation—Frees a child for only a part of the period of minority, or from only a part of the parent's rights, or for some purposes, and not for others. Also known as partial emancipation.

Single Parent Family—A family in which one parent remains the primary caretaker of the children, and the children maintain little or not contact with the other parent.

Status Offender—A child who commits an act which is not criminal in nature, but which nevertheless requires some sort of intervention and disciplinary attention merely because of the age of the offender.

Suicide—The deliberate termination of one's existence.

Truancy—Wilful and unjustified failure to attend school by one who is required to attend.

BIBLIOGRAPHY AND ADDITIONAL READING

The ACLU Department of Public Education (Date Visited: April 2001) <http://www.aclu.org>.

Bernard, Thomas J., The Cycle of Juvenile Justice. New York, NY: Oxford University Press, 1992.

Besharov, Douglas J. Recognizing Child Abuse, A Guide for the Concerned. New York, NY: The Free Press, 1990.

Black's Law Dictionary, Fifth Edition. St. Paul, MN: West Publishing Company, 1979.

Burgess, Ann Wolbert, Child Trauma I, Issues and Research. New York, NY: Garland Publishing, Inc., 1992

The Center for Disease Control (Date Visited: April 2001) <http://www.cdc.gov>.

Davidson II, William S., Redner, Robin, Amdur, Richard L., and Mitchell, Christina M.,Alternative Treatments for Troubled Youth. New York, NY: Plenum Press, 1990.

The Death Penalty Information Center (Date Visited: April 2001) <http://www.essential.org/dpic/>.

Drug and Other Substance Use Among School Children in New York State. Albany, NY: New York State Division of Substance Abuse Services, 1990.

Gardner, Sandra, and Rosenberg, Gary, Teenage Suicide. Englewood Cliffs, NJ: Julian Messner, 1990.

Gelfman, Mary H. B., and Gutman, Jewel A.,How To Handle Student Discipline Cases.Philadelphia, PA: The Practical Lawyer, The American Bar Association, Volume 37, Number 6, Page 43, September 1991.

Helfer, Ray E., and Kempe, Ruth S. The Battered Child. Chicago, IL: The University of Chicago Press, 1987.

Insurance Institute for Highway Safety. (Date Visited: April 2001) <http://www.hwysafety.org/>.

Lang, Alan R.The Encyclopedia of Psychoactive Drugs, Alcohol, Teenage Drinking. New York, NY: Chelsea House Publishers, 1985.

Lang, Susan S., Teen Violence. New York, NY: Franklin Watts, 1991.

Layman, Richard, Current Issues, Volume 1, Child Abuse. Detroit, MI: Omnigraphics, Inc., 1990.

The Legal Status of Adolescents. Washington, DC: Department of Health and Human Services, 1980.

Lotz, Roy, Poole, Eric D., and Regoli, Robert M., Juvenile Delinquency and Juvenile Justice. New York, NY: Random House, 1985.

McCarthy, Francis Barry, and Carr, James G. ,Juvenile Law and Its Processes. Charlottesville, VA: The Michie Company, 1989.

Mnookin, Robert H., and Weisberg, D. Kelly, Child, Family and State. Boston, MA: Little, Brown and Company, 1989.

Mothers Against Drunk Driving (M.A.D.D.). (Date Visited: April 2001) <http://www.madd.org/>.

National Center for Juvenile Justice (Date Visited: April 2001) <http://www.ncjj.org/>.

National Driver Register. (Date Visited: April 2001) <http://www.nhtsa.dot.gov/people/perform/driver/>.

National Highway Traffic Safety Administration. (Date Visited: April 2001) <http://www.nhtsa.dot.gov/>.

Nazario, Thomas A., In Defense of Children. New York, NY: Charles Scribner's Sons, 1988.

Roberts, Albert R., Juvenile Justice: Policies, Programs, and Services. Chicago, IL: The Dorsey Press, 1989.

Russell, Alene Bycer and Trainor, Cynthia Mohr, Trends in Child Abuse and Neglect: A National Perspective. Denver, CO: The American Human Association, 1984.

Shireman, Charles H., Rehabilitating Juvenile Justice. New York, NY: Columbia University Press, 1986.

Simonsen, Clifford E., Juvenile Justice in America. New York, NY: Macmillan Publishing Company, 1991.

Sobie, Merril, The Creation of Juvenile Justice: A History of New York's Children's Laws. Albany, NY: The New York Bar Foundation, 1987.

Soler, Mark, An Introduction to Children's Rights. Chicago, IL: ABA Journal, American Bar Association, Page 52, December1, 1988.

Schwartz, Ira M., In Justice For Juveniles. Lexington, MA: D.C. Heath and Company, 1989.

Thornton, William E. Jr., Voigt, Lydia and Doerner, William G.,Delinquency and Justice. New York, NY: Random House, 1987.

The United States Department of Education (Date Visited: April 2001) <http://www.ed.gov>.

The United States Department of Education Educational Resources Information Center (Date Visited: April 2001) <askeric@ericir.syr.edu>.

United States Department of Health and Human Services, National Child Abuse and Neglect Data System (NCANDS) (Date Visited: April 2001) <http://www.acf.dhhs.gov/>.

United States Department of Justice (Date Visited: April 2001) <http://www.usdoj.gov/>.

Vito, Gennaro F. and Wilson, Deborah G., The American Juvenile Justice System. Beverly Hills, CA: Sage Publications, Inc., 1985.

Washton, Arnold M., and Boundy, Donna, Cocaine and Crack, What You Need to Know. Hillside, NJ: Enslow Publishers, Inc., 1989.